# Lost at the Mill

## Anne Jordan

Copyright © Anne Jordan 2024

The right of Anne Jordan to be identified as author of this work has been asserted by her in accordance with the Copyright, Designs and Patents Act 1988.

All rights reserved.

The characters and events portrayed in this book are fictitious. Any similarity to real persons, living or dead, is coincidental and not intended by the author.

No part of this publication may be reproduced or transmitted in any form or by any means, electronic or mechanical, including photocopy, recording, or any information storage and retrieval system, without permission in writing from the publisher.

Cover/interior design by Liz Carter

This book is dedicated to Home for Good, a Christian charity with a Biblical mandate to care for vulnerable children. Home for Good is dedicated to finding a home for every child who needs one.

See homeforgood.org.uk

# Contents

| | |
|---|---:|
| Chapter One | 7 |
| Chapter Two | 14 |
| Chapter Three | 23 |
| Chapter Four | 31 |
| Chapter Five | 43 |
| Chapter Six | 50 |
| Chapter Seven | 62 |
| Chapter Eight | 69 |
| Chapter Nine | 77 |
| Chapter Ten | 84 |
| Chapter Eleven | 91 |
| Chapter Twelve | 97 |
| Chapter Thirteen | 107 |
| Chapter Fourteen | 119 |
| Chapter Fifteen | 126 |
| Chapter Sixteen | 136 |
| Chapter Seventeen | 141 |
| Chapter Eighteen | 146 |
| Chapter Nineteen | 153 |
| Chapter Twenty | 161 |
| Chapter Twenty-One | 164 |
| Chapter Twenty-Two | 170 |
| Some Helpful History | 181 |
| About the Author | 187 |

# Chapter One

"Helen, Helen, wake up!" Anna yelled from the bedroom window to her twin sister, who was asleep in bed. "Helen, get up! The whole world's gone white."

Helen groaned and turned over. Anna sighed. Why did her sister want to sleep on such a brilliant morning? She could not understand it.

A sudden thud of heavy snow falling from a tree had just woken Anna up. Peeping out of the curtains, she saw so much more snow than there had been yesterday. It covered every red berry on the holly bush at the bottom of the garden. Only the top half of the garden shed could be seen. Everything was a delicious meringue-white, still and perfect.

The ten-year-old Price twins were staying with their grandparents in their Victorian house in Keighley. They had come with their parents to stay for Christmas. On Christmas Day there had been no snow, but on Boxing Day it began, tiny flakes of snow dancing down then followed by even more flakes. It hadn't stopped snowing since. And now they couldn't get home, as the village was snowed in. How wonderful to not have to go back to school!

Grandad Price had grumbled for days. "Blooming newspapers are saying that the end of 1962 and the start of next year could be a really bad winter. Aye, that may be, but 1947 were…"

Anna had stopped listening. 1947 was in the olden days anyway.

It was so cold that the lake nearby had frozen over. That meant only one thing – skating. Fortunately, they had brought their skates with them. Oh, the feel of crisp cold air whooshing around them as they twirled around, with no fears or worries, even though their mum had told them to stay close to the edge. They had ignored her advice and skated right out to the centre and back. There were others doing the same; some of them were even grown-ups.

That was before the accident.

That had changed things.

Helen had fallen and sprained her ankle.

Mother had fussed around her in over-dramatic tones. After all, she was Amelia Price, the once-famous actress, who had followed her own mother onto the stage. The twins often found themselves embarrassed by her.

Anna could hear her mother now. "You must not go out now, darlings. It is so, so slippy. Your poor little feet. You must have perfect tootsies for when—"

"*Tootsies!*" Anna cried out loud now. "*Toes.* Why can't she say toes?"

"What?" groaned a voice from under a pile of blankets.

"Oh, you're alive then?" Anna said with just a tinge of sarcasm.

Helen yawned. She reached her hand out to her new watch on her bedside table. It was a Christmas present and had a real red leather strap – she had lost her other one at the swimming baths. Rubbing one eye then the other, she peered at her watch. "It's only seven-thirty, go away! It's Sunday, everyone has a lie in."

"There's been more snow in the night," Anna replied. "Heaps more."

"Well, so what? We're not allowed out of the house anyway." Helen let out another wide yawn.

"Just come and look. And anyway, I have a plan for us to get out."

"Really. How?

"Come and look first."

There was nothing for it. Sliding her feet out of bed and wrapping her eiderdown round her, Helen shuffled towards the window and looked out. She gasped – Anna was right! So much snow; it reached as far as she could see, all brilliant white. A cloudless blue sky stretched above it all.

She stood completely still, transfixed at the scene below. A milkman carrying a crate of milk was pushing his way forward on skis. As he stopped at each house in turn, he slid the skis to one side and bent over to pull bottles of milk from the crate, placing them by the front steps of each house. A nurse pushed her bicycle along the middle of the road, and a group of men shovelled drifts of snow to help her get through. Helen laughed at the sight of them slipping over and scrambling up again.

She thought of the lake at the park. Oh, how she wished she was there. She knew she wouldn't fall again – she was brilliant at skating, and Anna was too. Falling and twisting her ankle had just been one of those things. And anyway, she was better now. She turned to her sister. "Perfect," she sighed. "I need to be out there. So, what's the plan?"

"Escape now, before everyone gets up. We'll tiptoe down the stairs. Have a quick breakfast then out the front door. And, just to please you, how about dressing up?"

"Oh, you mean the stuff in the trunk in the kitchen?"

Anna smiled. "Yes, I just remembered it."

Grandma had shown them the trunk when they arrived. Anna had asked why it was there and not in the hall where you would expect it to be, and Grandma said it had been there when they bought the house. It was just part of the kitchen. If they wanted to play dressing up there were some old dresses in it, she'd said, some rather nice ones. It was a mystery as to how they got there. "Mystery clothes in the trunk?" Helen had said after Grandma left the kitchen. "How exciting! Maybe they belonged to a princess who was locked in a castle."

"Doubt it," Anna had replied. "Reckon Grandma just made it up so we could play silly games."

"You never know." Helen, unlike Anna, liked pretending.

Then Christmas came, and there were plenty of presents, then the snow and, best of all, skating. The trunk had been forgotten – until now.

Anna waited for Helen to say what she thought about her idea. Helen rubbed her chin and then gave a wide grin. "Dressing up – lovely!" she said. "We would look fabulous in posh dresses. Just imagine twirling on the ice, feeling the cold air rush around our ears, and... oh no! I just thought, what about—"

"I know. Grandad," Anna interrupted.

"Yes. Just suppose he gets up and sees us?" Helen frowned.

They both knew that Grandad had a habit of getting up early. After sneaking outside into the garden for a quick cigarette, he would hurry back to bed again, hoping he hadn't been seen. Grandma did not approve of Grandad smoking.

"We can tell him we are planning a poetry evening, and we are dressing up for it. It's not lying, because we could do one on New Year's Eve."

Mother was keen on them learning poetry.

"A poetry evening. Time to show off," said Helen. She cleared her throat and began reciting one she knew by heart. "'*How doth the little crocodile improve his shining tail—*'"

"No, not that one, it gives me nightmares." Anna shuddered at the thought of crocodile teeth, knife-sharp and hungry for human flesh.

"Ah, but poetry feeds the soul," Helen announced, throwing her arms in the air as her actress mother would.

"Hush, you'll end up with a flippin' Oscar," said Anna.

Helen did a mock bow.

# Chapter Two

It didn't take them long to get dressed and have a quick, quiet wash in cold water. After a quick brushing of teeth they were ready. No one stayed long in Grandma's draughty bathroom in winter.

"Tootsies ready," whispered Helen, grinning at her sister.

Anna nodded but didn't grin. She was the elder twin and the sensible one. Escaping was serious business. "First thing we do is tiptoe past Mum and Dad's bedroom."

Together they set off, hand in hand, stopping once to hold their breath as a floorboard squeaked. Their grandparents' room was next. As they tiptoed past, they heard Grandad snoring piggy snores.

Helen wanted to laugh, but a warning look from Anna stopped her.

A plaque with some words from the Bible hung on the wall next to the bedroom door. Grandma was the one who went to church. She had read it out loud to them one day: "In all your ways acknowledge Him, and He shall direct your paths. Proverbs 3 verse 6." She had talked about what it meant, but they didn't listen. They had tried going to church for a while, but it was boring so they stopped going. Not enough action; just sitting still all the time. But now if there was too much action they might be heard.

They reached the top of the stairs a few moments later and paused. Going downstairs was risky, as the old stairs creaked easily, so they took it slowly, only a few of the treads giving a slight groan.

Anna inched the kitchen door open a bit at a time, bracing herself for its squeak.

"Phew, we've made it," whispered Helen, pulling the door closed.

"Yes. I haven't held my breath so long for ages," gasped Anna, turning to the fridge. "Breakfast, then we go."

Grandma had kept up with the modern way of doing things in the sixties; she had bought a fridge.

"Not everyone has one," she'd said with just a touch of snobbery. Not that it was needed right now. For the past few days the milk had been frozen at the top when it was brought in.

Helen filled the kettle to make tea for them both, keeping silent to please her sister. Anna got the milk and found some slices of bread. They sat down to a simple breakfast of thick slices of toast and homemade plum jam washed down with a pot of tea.

"We'd better clear up," Anna said, collecting the plates and then washing up in silence, trying not to let the crockery clash together and make too much noise.

"Right, now for the mysterious trunk," said Helen, wiping the table. "I want to look in it first."

"Alright, but be quiet," Anna urged.

The trunk sat by the door to the back garden. Helen bent to lift the lid but then stopped. "It's really old, isn't it? Look at the wood, all knotty like a tree. And the brown is not the same all over. Bet it's heavy to lift."

Opening the lid was even harder than she thought. It creaked with each move, making her pause in case they were overheard. Carefully, bit by bit she eased it up until it was fully open. They both peered in. It was as Grandma had said: full of dresses. Helen pulled the top one out. "Just look at this!" She held it to her body, sighing. "It's the sort of thing women wore in the 1800s."

"Yes, and someone must have looked beautiful in this," Anna replied, taking the next dress out. She held it against her, admiring its gold-and-rose-coloured material and the tiny stitches.

Just then a nearby church clock chimed the hour, bringing them back to the present. "Oh no! Eight o'clock, we've got to hurry. They'll be getting up soon."

Helen snapped to attention. "Right. We put on the next two dresses we see and put these ones back." She reached into the trunk and took out the next dress. Unfolding it, she held it up. "Oh… that's not very pretty."

"It's a maid's uniform," said Anna. "Don't you remember that play mother was in? Can't remember what it was called. It was supposed to be wartime, and she was the kitchen maid." Anna grabbed it and held it next to her body. It fitted perfectly, as did the cap with it.

"They must have had small maids in those days," giggled Helen.

"Look, there's another one underneath." Anna took it out. "Same size and everything – and shoes too."

"Just right for us," said Helen, grinning. "Let's change into them. We can be two maids skating on the lake and doing curtsies."

It took only a few minutes for them to remove their own clothes, stow them in the trunk and pull the maid costumes on, complete with caps. They stood and faced each other; their way of finding out how they looked. "Wonderful," they said together.

"Only… won't we be cold, going outside in them?" said Helen, remembering the nurse she had seen wrapped up in her warm cloak.

"No, we'll put our wellies on in the hall and grab our skates. Then go out the front door without making a noise. Then we will run and jump and slide ourselves all the way to the lake. How's that for keeping warm?"

"Fantastic," said Helen. "Yes, and we won't fall over once."

"Ready?"

"Yes."

Tiptoeing towards the kitchen door together, they managed to reach it without making a sound. Anna put her hand out towards the handle then stopped, her hand frozen in space. "Hush... I heard a noise... footsteps? No, wait... I'm not sure."

Helen froze. "Footsteps, and us looking like this?"

"I'm not certain... can't be Grandad, he doesn't usually come into the kitchen. Just stay put. Like I said, we're planning a poetry evening and we are dressing up for it."

"Suppose it's not. Suppose it's one of the others," whispered Helen.

"*You're* the actress. Oh, wait..." Anna, paused, her finger to her lips, "...it *is* footsteps, and they are getting closer."

There was nothing they could do but stand very still and hope it was Grandad.

The footsteps stopped; the door handle turned. It wasn't Grandad. Staring directly at them was a tall, unsmiling woman, a complete stranger, dressed in a long, wide black dress with a white apron round her waist. Her neat grey-black hair was pulled back over her ears in a low bun, a spotless white cap tied under her chin. One hand was in her pocket, the other behind her back.

Looking them up and down, she tut-tutted and shook her head. "Took your time getting here, didn't you?"

Neither Anna nor Helen answered, both too shocked to speak.

"And insolent, too."

Despite having no idea who this woman was, the twins heard themselves say "Sorry," one after the other.

"You both look a bit small to be old enough to be maids. Still, there are two of you. Twins, I guess? Four good legs for running up and down the stairs. Cook is ill, and the scullery maid had to go home as her mother is dying, so there's a lot to do."

Anna and Helen had no idea what to say next, so they remained silent.

"Humph, workhouse manners, I shouldn't wonder. I am the housekeeper here. When I speak, you answer, 'Yes, Mrs. Dreary.' You must always look at me so I can see if you are telling the truth. Do you understand?"

"Yes, Mrs Dreary," Anna and Helen repeated parrot fashion.

"But you must never raise your eyes to anyone above your station. By that I mean the master of the house and his business friends. Right. As new maids, these are your duties."

Then followed a long list of what they were required to do. This ended with a reminder of the first thing on the list, which was to bring the coal up from the cellar and clean and relay the fires.

Both Anna and Helen managed a stuttered "Yes, Mrs. Dreary."

"You must speak clearly. I'm not deaf, mind; it's just everyone mutters these days. Right – no time to lose." Turning on her heels, she left the room with a grand exit.

Anna and Helen were left alone. Neither of them moved or spoke.

Eventually, Helen let out a sigh. "Wasn't she just marvellous? I mean – all those lines. It must have taken her ages to learn them."

"How do you mean?" Anna asked.

"Can't you guess? She's probably one of Mother's acting friends."

"What?"

"One of Mother's acting friends," Helen repeated. "Mother got her to come to give us a scare, just like she did last year. Remember when she got that pretend policeman to come before Christmas to arrest us for not being good?"

"Yes, but I'm not sure it's one of Mother's acting friends this time. How did she get into the house? The doors are locked. Everyone is still asleep... and also, where is she now?"

"You don't think she's a…"

"A ghost? No." Anna shook her head at the very idea of it. "You know I don't believe in ghosts. Anyway, I could hear her breathing fast, as though she had been rushing around. There *is* something strange about it all, though."

"Oh, how lovely, a mystery play. Mother has arranged it somehow to cheer us up." Helen clapped her hands as if she was watching it on stage. "Maybe there is a dead body in the broom cupboard. I'm going to look."

"No! Don't turn around." Anna began to make for the door.

Helen stood still. "Why, are you scared?" Not waiting for an answer, she turned around. "What?" Her mouth dropping open in shock, she could only stare. "The trunk… it's gone! And… and… oh, it can't be! Everything else, too."

Anna now had an inkling of what was happening. It was no good; she had to look. She turned around, and like her sister she could only stare. The kitchen, with all its modern appliances, had gone. The old heavy trunk had gone too.

Everything had completely changed.

# Chapter Three

Anna knew exactly what had happened. She also knew – as only a twin could – what her sister would say next. "No, it isn't," she said before Helen had time to speak.

"But it has to be. It just *has* to be a stage set," said Helen, tears gathering in the corners of her eyes. "I mean… it can't be anything else. That lady we saw must have pressed something. It all came when we weren't looking."

Anna shook her head. "The only way to know exactly what has happened is to touch everything."

"All right, but… but it's a stage set. I just know it is."

Anna didn't reply. She knew when not to argue with Helen. Instead she stepped over to where the fridge had been and where there now stood an open-shelved cabinet containing a number of different sized copper pans. Anna reached out her hand and took hold of one of them, then handed it to Helen. "Feel that."

Helen took it silently, stroking her hand over the copper and frowning. She stared at the space it left and then picked up the other pans in turn, squinting at the space behind them.

"They're not cardboard," Anna said. "They are solid, heavy pans, real old ones. Someone has polished them. You can see your face in them."

"It's clever," Helen said, "but there must be a door or a flap or something." She poked around the kitchen frantically, seeking some clue to it all. Searching in corners, jumping on the floor and pushing at things – but there were no trap doors. Nothing. It was all solid and real.

Anna watched. It was awful to see her sister so upset.

"What has happened to us?" Helen whispered, standing still at last.

"We will know for sure when we look out of the window," replied Anna.

Helen shrugged and turned to the window. Anna stood back a little to allow her to look out. Helen froze in place – it just couldn't be true! "The snow, it's gone, all of it! It can't do that. I mean… there's no snow at all!"

Anna peered over her sister's shoulder. It was as she expected. No snow, nothing. Nothing to suggest there even might have been recently. The grass was a dirty shade of green. The trees were bare, their branches black against a grey winter sky. As she stood, a thin, chilly breeze moaned through a tiny gap at the bottom of the window frame. "Have you guessed what's happened?"

Helen nodded her head, her face white with shock. "But it's just so mind blowing."

"I know… but it's true. I knew it the moment I saw the housekeeper go." Anna's voice trembled a little.

"The housekeeper?"

"Yes. She had her hands behind her back, and in them were a bunch of keys," replied Anna. "I've seen them before, in Grandad's shed. You were there when he said he had dug up some old things in the garden?"

"Yes, it was boring."

"Well, one day he showed me them. He had found out from a book that the keys were Victorian."

"Victorian?"

"Yes. The maid's costumes must have belonged to some real Victorian maids. By putting them on we have somehow gone back to Victorian times."

"It's just so incredible. I still can't take it in," said Helen.

"I know."

Helen neither moved nor spoke.

"Helen, don't you understand? We... you and me... are now real maids. And we had better get that coal, or—"

Helen didn't stop to hear what Anna was going to say next. She sprang towards the door and shoved through, not caring if she was heard. Anna tried to catch her up, but Helen was too quick. Racing towards the front door, she yanked it open and ran down the front steps to the pavement. She skidded to a halt, and there Anna joined her. "What are you doing?"

"I have to make sure," Helen panted.

"Alright then. Let's have a good look around."

Helen went one way and Anna the other. Both of them walked slowly, taking their time as they gazed at everything around, above, and below them. Then they turned and came back to the house, almost at the same time, and looked at each other.

"Yes. It's definitely true, but I can't take it in… it's unbelievable. I'm usually the one who makes things up." Helen shook her head, looking as if a mountain had just fallen in front of her.

Anna nodded. "But why? That's the bit I don't get."

"Me too… but suddenly I feel so much better. This is a real adventure, better even than skating on the lake!"

Anna didn't answer. She'd caught the edge of a strange smell, drifting towards them. The sky darkened, and billows of smoke began to rise into the sky. In an instant, they both knew what it was. "Fire!" they cried out together.

"It must be the old people's home," Helen cried. "We must get them out."

They had seen the home on the day they arrived. "River View Home for the elderly," Grandad had said as he drove them past it. "You won't get me in one of those."

And now it was on fire.

They set off running down the road.

"Helen…" panted Anna a few minutes later, "…Grandad said it was new. It… it's Victorian times now, so it will be… something… else."

Helen tried to speak but couldn't as she was out of breath. She stumbled as they continued down the road, which curved downwards towards the river. They could now see flames, bright against the skyline. Helen suddenly stopped, clutching her side, and then she sank to the ground. "I don't think I can make it."

Anna helped her sister up. "Put your arm around my waist. We can run a bit then stop."

"I'll try."

As they made their faltering way down the hill they began to see things more clearly. Flames licked the sides of a building, which they could now see wasn't the old people's home. This was a much larger building with a large chimney. Billows of red and yellow flames were reaching towards the chimney and spreading fast.

They could not get too close, as the smoke was choking them and making them feel dizzy. Several fire engines were gathered around the area. To Helen and Anna, they looked very different from modern-day fire engines. A number of firemen were frantically pumping water from the river, spraying it at the building as fast as they could, then going back for more. But it did little to put the flames out.

The fire was spreading rapidly, blotting out the sun in the sky.

"Fetch some water!" a firemen called out to the crowd of people gathered nearby. "Stand back. Watch out! That bit of wall is about to go!"

It was no use. More of the building had caught fire, chunks of masonry and wood falling to the ground with loud thuds. Horses whinnied and women cried, covering their faces with their hands. Children cowered behind their mothers.

Anna watched as a man in a top hat shoved his way through the crowd. "Get out of the way! My mill's on fire," he yelled. "Save me mill!"

The crowd parted to let him through.

In no time at all the entire mill was on fire. No amount of water could put it out now.

"Stand back, everyone. Nowt can save it," a fireman shouted.

It was true. The whole of the building was crumbling. Nothing could save it. Everyone stood back and watched as the roaring fire did its worst.

Anna and Helen backed away up a grassy hill to a safe distance, following some of the others from the crowd. Suddenly, out of all the noise and pandemonium, a young girl of around their own age came running towards them, her long, wild, black curly hair flying around her face. She stopped and stood in front of them. Her clothes reeked of smoke and were covered in soot. She looked in a sorry state. She pushed her hair away from her face, and Anna and Helen could see her more clearly. Her soft, beautiful brown eyes with a hint of gold looked sad. Her dark skin was sweaty and dirty from having been close to the fire. "My name is Connie Abara," she said. "I need your help, please. Do not go, please. I must leave this place now. Please say you will help me."

She said no more but stood very still, her eyes pleading for help.

# Chapter Four

Helen was the first to speak. "Are you alright?"

Connie nodded. "I am not hurt… but I must go. I must find what Mother told me to look for. You are maids, so you are good girls, yes? You will come with me?"

Anna had never heard anyone so young speak almost like a grown-up. She could see by the look of awe on her sister's face that she was thinking the same.

"You are quiet," Connie said. "Is it because I am from another country?"

"No!" Anna replied quickly.

"I will tell you my story. It will help you understand. We will sit. It is warm with the heat from the fire."

Connie sank onto the grassy ground, and Anna and Helen sat down together next to her. The fire was still raging below. People were leaving now, many in shocked silence. The man in the top hat was sitting on the grass, just staring at where the mill had been.

Connie began to speak. "It is bad. I had a job at the mill, but now because of the fire it is lost. But worse still… my… my mother died this morning."

Anna and Helen were too shocked to speak.

Connie blinked. "I can see you are both upset. Mother always told me to be brave and not cry… but it is hard."

"But it's awful, you have no one to give you a hug," said Helen.

Connie did not reply. She looked away, swallowing, and Anna and Helen could see tears spilling from her eyes and down her cheeks. Helen shuffled nearer to Connie on one side, and Anna on the other, and they linked arms together behind her back like a cradle then closed their eyes.

Soon they heard quiet sobs. They sat silently as Connie wept between them, her body trembling.

After some time Connie wiped her hand over her eyes. "Thank you," she said, sniffling. The girls smiled gently at her, and without saying a word shifted back to where they were sitting before. No one spoke for quite a while.

It was Anna who broke the silence. She felt she had to say something. "Were you working there when the fire began?"

"It's Sunday, the Sabbath. No one works on the Sabbath."

"Oh, yes, sorry. So it is… sorry." Anna felt her face going red.

"It is alright. I will carry on with my story. My mother lived in South Africa with my grandfather. They came from England. They were rich. Grandfather bought things from African men to sell in England. My mother fell in love with an African man Grandfather knew."

"How romantic," sighed Helen.

"Ah, but Grandfather wouldn't let them get married, so they ran away to England. They got married, and a year later I was born."

"Did you come here to Keighley to begin with?" asked Anna, trying to sound intelligent after making the mistake about the Sabbath.

"Yes," replied Connie. "When my mother was young, she was sent to a boarding school near here. Mother was taught how to be a lady. Mother always said I too am a lady."

"Ah, yes… right," said Anna.

"When we came here, we only had a bit of money," Connie continued, "but Father earned enough for us to live in a house and buy food. He worked down a mine."

"Oh, how horrible," said Helen. "To be under the ground day after day in the darkness, never to see the sun."

"Yes, but then… then last month there was an accident. Father was killed…" Connie stopped, staring up at the sky, her eyes brimming with more tears, "…and there was no money then, so Mother and I went to work in the mill. We had to, so we could buy food."

"That must have been awful," Anna said.

"Yes. Then just last week Mother got sick, and this morning she died. Mother has gone. My wages have gone, too."

"Is there no one in your house?" asked Anna.

"I have no brothers and sisters. It is only me. But I think I have a relative nearby. Mother whispered something when she was dying – it sounded like, "Look for May." Then she said, "Maccle." I think it was that. I have not been outside Keighley at all. If you know where Maccle is, then will you please take me there?"

Anna looked at Helen. Each knew the other one was stuck for something to say.

"You don't know a place called Maccle?" Connie asked after a short silence.

"No... er.... sorry," Anna replied.

Anna knew that Helen wanted her to say more. She could tell from the way Helen raised her eyebrows. But how could she say that they were from a different time and they were not real maids? She thought some more. Best to keep it simple. "We have never been outside Keighley, either."

Helen simply nodded.

"Oh, that is a pity," sighed Connie. "There is something else, too. Just before Mother died, she lifted her hand and pointed to the bottom of the door..." Connie stopped for a moment, brushing a single tear from her cheek, "...I wondered if she meant the floor by the door. I went over and bent down to look. One of the floorboards was a bit loose. I hadn't noticed it before. I tried to lift it, but it was too hard to move. So I got a knife from the kitchen and bit by bit I lifted it up. Then I saw this." Connie reached into her dress pocket and drew something out, then she opened her hand for them to look.

"Oh, how beautiful," gasped Helen.

Lying flat on Connie's hand was a purse, trimmed in lace with a drawstring top, embroidered with birds and red roses. White daisies made of tiny beads were arranged in two rows at the bottom. The purse was both delicate and beautiful.

"Your mother was a real lady," said Helen.

"I told you she was."

"Oh yes... sorry, I didn't mean she wasn't, but this is something like it belongs to... a princess or..." Helen trailed off.

"Maybe it was a present from someone?" Anna said quickly, trying to be more down to earth than her sister.

"I thought that too," replied Connie. "Maybe my father bought it for her birthday. He liked to buy her things. When I saw it, I looked at it for a long time. I want to be a lady like my mother when I grow up."

"So do I. And be rich," said Helen.

Anna said nothing. All she wanted to do when she grew up was to live in the country and keep chickens.

For a few seconds the three of them looked at the purse, forgetting all about the now dying fire below them. All the voices and noises around them seemed to fade into the distance.

"Do you want to see what's inside it?" Connie asked, breaking the silence.

"Yes please," the twins answered together.

Connie opened the purse and shook the contents into her lap. There they lay for all to see. Connie picked them up in turn. A shiny purple necklace, a lace handkerchief, a green ribbon, a large bird's feather, a lock of hair, a small triangular flat pebble and a folded piece of paper.

"It must be all her treasures," said Helen. "Look at the necklace – reckon those purple bits are some kind of real jewels, and the green ribbon must be real velvet… and the lace must be real too. I expect your mother was keeping the necklace for you to wear when you are a lady, and the ribbon and the lace too."

Anna wasn't looking at any of those things. She was looking at the lock of hair. It was black, thick, and curly. "Is it your hair?"

"No," said Connie. "My father's. He had very tight curls, lots more than me."

The handkerchief and feather were stroked and admired. Connie held the pebble in the palm of her hand for a moment. "This is quite pretty too."

Just then the man in the top hat strode past them, muttering about his mill and how all was now lost and he was ruined. A sudden gust of wind blew his hat off and towards where they sat. He charged after it. Anna picked it up and handed it to him. The man took the hat and put it on his head but neither smiled nor said thank you. Anna watched him go, only to see the hat flying off once again. This time he grabbed it but did not put it back on his head. Anna watched him walk away. "Is he the boss… I mean master?"

"Yes, that is the mill owner, Mr. Cooper," Connie replied. "He is not a good man. He hits people. He fines some people if they talk or look out of the window. Sometimes if people are late he fines them too."

"How horrible," said Helen.

"Yes," said Anna, "he looks nasty."

An old, bent-over woman was following behind him. Glancing over at Connie, she snarled, "Aye, lass, thee won't find work now, not you with a face like a jellied eel." She walked away, cackling.

"That was horrible too," Helen said.

Anna agreed. "Awful."

Connie nodded. "Insults I can take, but accidents are a different thing. It sometimes happens if you are very tired at the end of the day. Sometimes your hair gets caught in the machines and tears it out and—"

"Should we look at the folded paper now?" interrupted Helen, who was the most squeamish twin. "I wonder what it says?"

"I haven't opened it," said Connie, "because I was frightened it might say something bad about my mother and father. Some people at the mill said bad words to my mother about my father. It made Mother cry."

"They shouldn't do that," said Anna. "Calling people names is always bad." The twins had sometimes been called names at school by the 'in' gang. It was just because they both had red hair.

Helen nodded in agreement. She was thinking about the gang too.

Connie took the paper from her lap. "Mother taught me how to read. Mother said reading means you will never be lonely."

"So does it say anything about Maccle or May or where Maccle is?" asked Anna.

Connie didn't answer. Instead, she began to read out the words in front of her: "In all your ways acknowledge Him, and He shall direct your paths. Proverbs 3 verse 6."

Helen gasped. "That's amazing! It's the same Bible verse as the one on Grandma's—"

Anna gave a slight shake of her head, and Helen stopped.

"You have a grandmother?" asked Connie.

"Oh, yes, but not here." Anna looked down at the ground. If only Connie knew the truth.

"I sometimes wish I had a grandmother." Connie looked sad for a moment, then she brightened. "But now we have God on our side. The piece of paper is a sign. You both have been sent to me." Connie scooped the objects into her purse and jumped to her feet. "We must go now... please... or they will take me."

"Take you where?" Anna asked.

"When they find out my mother has died, they will try to take me to the workhouse. Mother told me that's where children go when they have no one to look after them. I cannot go back to my house."

Both twins knew what a workhouse was. Mother had once acted the part of Nancy from *Oliver Twist*. For a second neither of them spoke.

"You are both silent. So you know how terrible the workhouse is. Mother would not want that to happen to me."

Up till now, Anna had felt doubtful about getting involved in something she knew nothing about. But here was a real Victorian orphan, waiting for an answer. They had only known Connie for a short time, but she had opened her heart to them. She had no home, no money, no parents. How could they say no?

The three of them got to their feet and looked at each other, waiting for someone to speak.

"We don't have much to go on," said Anna finally. "A place called Maccle and a name – May – but we will try. Yes, we will come. We will do what we can." She saw Helen nod and smile. "I am Anna, and this is my twin sister Helen. We are your friends now."

"Thank you," said Connie.

"So, where do we begin?" Helen asked.

"We ask God to show us the right path."

"How?"

"We say a prayer, of course. Mother would want me to. Don't you say your prayers?"

"Oh, yes, we say prayers," Helen said and, ignoring a sideways kick from Anna, she began, "For what we are about to receive… abide with me, and… all things bright and beautiful and… and give us strength as… as… we bravely go. God save the Queen. Amen."

The *Amen* was said so triumphantly that both Connie and Anna gave a hearty *Amen* to it. After all, thought Anna, Helen had courage even though she didn't know any prayers.

As they opened their eyes, the three of them turned their backs on the remains of the dreadful fire that had brought them all together.

# Chapter Five

"Where do we begin? Anna asked.

"Before we look for Maccle, first we should go into town," said Connie. "Then to Uncle Barney's."

"Oh right, good idea," said Helen, ignoring one of Anna's looks, as though she had known Uncle Barney all her life.

Connie led Helen and Anna to the road leading into town. They were not the only ones who had begun to walk away. Many of the others were women, their faces pale and shocked as they made their way to the road. Leaving the men to put the fire out completely, their whole world in ashes, they hugged their children to their sides.

The sad procession made its way towards the town. Connie and the twins walked on, silent now.

The town, with its many tall factory chimneys, looked grey. A heavy, choking, smoky stench that seemed to be oozing from the factories began to settle on their bodies.

They were met by folk running towards them. It was clear from the solemn looks on their faces that they had seen – or smelt – the smoke from the fire. Some just watched from afar and shook their heads. Some handed out chunks of bread and mugs of watered-down beer, which were received gratefully. Connie and the twins sat by the side of the road to eat their bread and drink their beer. The twins were grateful, even though the beer tasted more like stewed tea.

"Now to Uncle Barney's," Connie said after they had finished. She got up and brushed some crumbs away from her dress.

Neither Anna nor Helen replied. The seriousness of it all was beginning to sink in. This was real and it was horrible.

Connie led them a little further down the road, then turned into a small, dismal courtyard. She stopped at a shop entrance. Anna and Helen simply stood and looked at it, feeling one another's disgust at the sight in front of them. On the ground to one side of the doorway lay a vile smelling heap of recent dog vomit. Helen put her hand over her nose. Anna took a few quick steps backwards into the street. Then she saw a sign above the shop: 'Barney Cheap, Pawn Broker.' Through the grimy windows she could just make out a jumble of all sorts of items.

Some tarnished teaspoons sat next to some battered pans. Piles of worn blankets languished in a forlorn heap next to some old coats. Several old tools lay in front of them. Strings of beads and other bits of jewellery were scattered next to an array of cotton and lace handkerchiefs. And there was more stuff in untidy heaps.

Anna remembered what a pawn shop was. The twins had seen Mother acting in *Oliver Twist* twice. A pawn shop was where you sold something that belonged to you for money in return.

The door was slightly open. Connie took the purse out of her pocket and started towards it. In an instant Anna knew what Connie was about to do – she was going to sell the necklace. Anna shot a glance at Helen, who mouthed, *"Stop her!"*

Grabbing hold of Connie's arm, Anna pulled her back. "No, not that. Not the necklace."

"But we will need a shawl each to keep us warm. It's cold now that we are away from the fire."

"Yes… but not the necklace."

"Anna's right," said Helen. "Look, it might be worth lots of money. When you find your new home, you can sell it then and live off the money."

Connie shrugged. "Yes, alright then, I suppose so. Maybe the handkerchief… and the ribbon. Yes, we will try them instead." She made for the door again and went in. Anna and Helen made no objection and followed her.

The first thing the twins were aware of was how dark it was. One single candle burned on the counter, the air heavy and damp, hanging like a death-shroud.

Uncle Barney popped his head above the counter. With dried bits of food in his moustache, he looked a sorry sight as he stood up and frowned at the three girls. He shifted his gaze around the room. "Uncle Barney does no stealin' now. Uncle Barney does charity." Then, as though he hadn't seen children before, he bent his head forward and stared into their faces. "Well, strike us dead. Nowt but nippers, two maids an' a flippin'—'

Anna burst in quickly, "Good morning, Mr. Uncle… Cheap. We would like to buy three shawls in exchange for these two fine things." Taking the handkerchief and ribbon from Connie's open hand, she put them down on the counter.

Just then the door opened, and someone came in. "Don't mind waiting," a voice called out.

Uncle Barney took no notice. Staring at the handkerchief and ribbon, he began to chuckle. "Well, blow me head off. Eee, them looks like real ladies' fings. Can't say I sees them often." Laughing louder now, Uncle Barney's nose began to drip with wet snot, making Anna turn her head away in disgust. Helen and Connie drew back a couple of steps.

A sudden blast of Uncle Barney's bad breath began to weave around them all. Choking out one final snort and wiping his nose on his sleeve, he straightened up and did a little bow. "Eee, lass, tha' has manners. I don't see that much in 'ere. An so I should say too. Uncle Barney likes a bit of respect. Reet then, it's shawls is it? Well, I 'aint got any. But yer can 'ave that best blanky over there. An' I tells yer what, I'll cut it up into three fer yer. I'll get yer it." Muttering to himself, he shuffled across to where the blankets lay and scrabbled through the pile, drawing out a faded blue one. Blowing the dust off, he held the blanket up for them to see. "Reet then, now look at this – no 'oles, an' warm wool. Uncle Barney does no stealin' now. Uncle Barney does charity."

Anna turned to look at Connie and Helen, who both nodded their heads. True, there were no holes, although the blanket looked thin in places. Anna had a sudden thought and looked Uncle Barney straight in the eye. "It's got no... er... germs, has it?"

"Nah, lass, Uncle Barney does no germs. I says no to germs. Fine blanky that, left 'ere over a year ago. That Mrs never come back fer it, so mine to sell, see."

"Oh, thank you, Uncle... er, Mr. Cheap," Anna said, glancing at Connie and Helen, who both nodded. "We will take it if you'll cut it up for us, please."

"Never say no to a lady, Uncle Barney doesn't. Now, where's them scissors?" He began to search the counter and then the floor, and Anna took the chance to peep over the top of the counter to watch him. The floor – or what might be a floor – had no space without something crowded into it. Stuff at one time having a use lay there in little heaps. She watched him scrambling about then retreated when she heard him cry, "Eee, got em." He took hold of the blanket and, folding it into three, cut it down each fold. He handed the makeshift shawls to Anna and grabbed the hanky and ribbon from the counter.

Without more ado, the three girls hurried out of the shop, colliding with a hooded person near the door, who grumbled something rude. Away up the courtyard they ran, relieved to be away from the grime, the stink and the dark shadows.

Anna had done her first bit of trading in Victorian times. But she was glad it was over.

# Chapter Six

"Thank you, Anna," Connie said, looking relieved that they were now all safely together in the main street.

"Is that your real uncle?" Helen asked.

"No, everyone calls him Uncle Barney. Pawnbrokers are always called 'Uncle'. Don't you know that?"

"Oh, yes... I mean, er... I wouldn't want *him* for an uncle."

"You might if you were hungry," Connie said, looking serious.

Anna didn't say anything; she thought it best not to. She was busy sorting out the blanket, handing out one piece to each of them. She wrapped her own new, raggedy shawl around her shoulders. "Well, these'll keep us warm, even though they look a bit strange."

"Yes, they will do until we get to Maccle." Connie smiled a grateful smile. "And now we must go. We will carry on up this road – it should lead us out of town."

Anna wanted to ask if there were any signposts nearby but stopped herself in time. Did they even exist in Victorian times? How could she find out? She pondered for a few seconds, then said, "Connie, er... are there any... like, stone things with name places on them? Like... it might say 'Maccle' on it, and then however many miles—" She stopped as the wind whipped off her cap, and bent to pick it up. But the wind kept blowing it away, and she ran up the hill after it. As she tried once again to grab hold of it, someone collided with her. She looked up. A bearded man wearing a dull brown coat, a black scarf and a hat that was so big it covered up most of his forehead stood there, looking at her. He kicked out with a long leg to stop the cap blowing further away then picked it up, bowed, and handed it to her. "Thank you," she said, staring up at him.

Peering at her more closely, he bowed again. "Sorry, signora, *mi scusi*, how you say, excuse knocking me to you. It is me not looking I was going."

His voice sounded foreign, Anna thought, maybe Italian. "Oh, that's alright," she replied, replacing her cap on her head the best she could.

"Also, signora, I found you say you was looking for Maccle. Only… I born there as a bambino."

"Oh, yes… we are looking for Maccle."

"I tell you way now. It is the road up," the man said, pointing further up the road. "Better more, I write for you."

Plucking a piece of paper and a pencil from his pocket, he scribbled a few words then nodded to himself, cleared his throat, and read them aloud. "You all walk up road to roads in a cross and turn left to bridge with a hump. It be a little way. Go past castle, through next field by footpath that goes to canal. Over bridge and walking on footpath then to see Maccle. It not far."

"Thank you," Anna said, accepting the piece of paper.

"As you say in this country, my wishes for a good morning." The man bowed again and walked away.

Helen and Connie caught up with Anna. "Who was that?" asked Helen.

"He didn't say who he was, but he heard us talking about Maccle. He sounded Italian. He said he was born there, in Maccle. He has written down some directions for us." She read them out falteringly. "Bit hard to follow," she said, folding the paper and sliding it into one of her apron pockets. "Guess he means us to carry on walking up this road to some crossroads."

"Yes, but it is a help," replied Connie. "We must go now so we get there in daylight." She began to stride off up the hill, and Anna and Helen had to run to keep up with her.

Anna looked down as she ran. It was harder to run on Victorian cobblestones, so different from the tarmac roads of the sixties. And it was not easy to run in a Victorian maid's dress. With one hand she hitched it up off the ground a little, not realising she was showing her ankles. She spotted some shocked looks from people passing by.

After a long stint of running, Connie began to slow down, and Anna and Helen breathed a sigh of relief as they trailed behind her, stopping to wrap their blankets around their heads as the wind got stronger. "This journey seems to be taking longer than the man said," Anna said to no one in particular. She glanced at Connie, who was staring ahead into the distance. She looked at Helen and noticed how pale she was. She was feeling either sick or hungry; Anna didn't know which.

Eventually some crossroads came into view, and they came to a stop, breathing heavily. "Whew," Helen gasped, bending over. "Can't walk another step. I've got a stitch in my side."

"A what?" Connie asked.

"Oh." Helen had forgotten she was now in Victorian times. "I forgot… no… I mean, I have a pain in the side of my body."

Connie pointed to the side of the road. "Let's just sit down by that hedge. I am sorry I went fast to begin with. It was the thought of a new home."

"That's alright," replied Helen, straightening up.

Slumping down by the hedge, they were all content to be quiet for a while, each lost in their own thoughts. Surprisingly it was Helen who spoke first. "I'm alright now."

Anna fished the directions out of her pocket and read them aloud again. "So, it looks like we turn left at the crossroads. That way," she said, pointing.

"Not far now," said Connie, scrambling to her feet and sprinting off at once with the others following in her wake.

As they ran, Anna began to feel uneasy. Was it just her imagination or something real? Something – or was it somebody – that wasn't right? A small curl of fear began to grow. She shook her head. Imagination, that's all it was.

"What did you shake your head for?" Helen whispered.

"Nothing – just a bit tired, that's all."

"So am I. Don't know when we're going to eat."

"We'll find something in Maccle." Anna, sounding more positive than she felt inside, began to run faster, grabbing hold of Helen's hand as they caught up with Connie. At least now they were out of town the air was fresher.

Just then Anna heard something. A rustle, maybe. It seemed to be coming from behind a nearby hedge. She was about to stop when she caught a glimpse of the bridge in front of them. Oh, at last! The directions were right, after all. All her earlier fears went out of her head. Beyond the bridge was the castle. Not far at all.

"The bridge with a hump," Helen called out excitedly, pointing ahead.

"At last," Connie said breathlessly. She stopped, holding her side. "I think I too have the stitch." Despite being exhausted, they all laughed. Connie's face fell for a moment. "I really should not laugh… but I think Mother in Heaven would not mind."

Anna and Helen stifled their laughter. "I think your mother would be happy to know you will soon have a home," Anna said gently.

"You have both been very kind. I am thinking I was expecting a lot of you both, to come with me. You are maids. Your mistress will be wondering where you are."

Helen nudged Anna a little, willing her to say something.

*In all your ways acknowledge Him, and He shall direct your paths.* A little voice whispered the words in Anna's head. "Oh," she said, jumping a little. "Those words from the Bible came into my head from nowhere. What could that mean?"
Connie opened her mouth to speak. "I think—"

"No." Helen held up her hand. "Stop. I think it means we have to carry on and God will help us."

Anna nodded and smiled. It was brave of Helen. But the curl of fear deep inside seemed to be getting bigger, making her shiver just a little.

Connie took hold of her hand. "You are cold… there is something wrong?"

Anna shrugged. "I don't know. But let's go." Not waiting for the others, she began to sprint towards the bridge, the others hurrying after her. As they ran Anna suddenly saw in her mind the man who had bumped into her. He was speaking once again, giving her directions to Maccle.

*"You all walk up road to roads in a cross and turn left to bridge with a hump. It be a little way. Go past castle, through next field by footpath that goes to canal. Over bridge and walking on footpath then to see Maccle. It not far."*

It all sounded fine. They had found the humpback bridge, and yet… something was wrong. But what was it? She stopped running, and Helen and Connie bumped into her. "Why have you stopped?" Helen asked.

"There's something wrong. I can feel it."

"How do you mean?" asked Connie.

"I just don't know, but a few minutes ago I thought I heard a rustle in the hedge."

"Oh," said Helen. "It might be a tiger, or a lion got loose from the—" She stopped mid-sentence as Anna gave her one of her looks.

But Connie's face had fallen into serious lines. "A lion *has* escaped from the circus. Mother told me about it. She heard it at the mill."

"Where was it? I mean, the circus?" asked Helen.

"They just go from one place to another. Do you not know about the circus?" Connie replied.

Helen nodded a few times. "Yes. I got mixed up… I meant the lion. Did it get caught?"

"Don't know. Maybe."

"Then it might be out there," Helen whispered, the colour draining from her face. Springing forward, she raced up the road, the others trying their best to keep up. She came to the bridge and sprinted over it. Anna called out to her to slow down, but Helen was having nothing of it. Past the castle and the field she ran. She did not stop until they were nearly at the canal. Completely exhausted, she sank to her knees, and Anna and Connie caught her up and crouched down with her.

"Are you alright?" Anna placed her arm around her sister's shoulders.

"No," said Helen, her voice breaking into a cry. "We might be eaten alive." Slumping over, she sobbed into her now dirty maid's dress.

Connie didn't speak but closed her eyes, her lips moving as if in silent prayer.

"Hey, over there!" a female voice suddenly yelled from a barge moored to the side of the canal. "Do yer need any 'elp?"

"Yes, yes, we do! My friends and I need somewhere to be safe from the lion," Connie called back.

"A lion? Oh, yes, the lion that ran off... come over 'ere. I'm Sally. Yer'll be safe with us. We have food and water, too."

Helen immediately stopped crying and raised her head slowly. Through bleary vision she could just make out the shape of a horse on the path by the barge. On the barge stood a scowling young man and an older woman, whom she took to be the young man's mother. The man turned away, shaking his head. Sally beckoned at them to come over.

"Thank you," Helen croaked, relieved. Not having a handkerchief, she rubbed her eyes a few times.

Connie led them to the barge, and Sally helped them climb on board. "Eee, I've never seen such miseries. Come inside the cabin an' get thee warm. Sally will get tha' victuals... an' never mind 'im, he's me own an' he says nowt to no one." Sally showed them inside, followed silently by her son. "There aint much room, so sits yersens down 'ere." She indicated a bit of floor space near the front of the barge.

Grateful to be out of the wind, they sank to the floor. It was a while before any of them could speak properly. "Thank you," Connie said. Anna waited for her breath to come back, then told Sally they had been running away from the mill.

"Aye, well, I heard about t'fire, bad thing that," Sally said, shaking her head. "But yer needn't be worried about that lion. It's bin caught, so that's done with."

Connie, taking another deep breath, told Sally where they were hoping to go. Sally raised her eyebrows then started to laugh. "Maccle? Yer goin' to Maccle? Eee, that's funny... oh, I mean, aye... well, maybe yer are so, but... *Maccle*..." Choking on her laughter now, Sally could say no more.

Anna wondered if the others were as puzzled as she was. Why was going to Maccle so funny? Was it not a good place? She decided it was best not to ask. It was up to Connie to make her own mind about it when they got there.

"Well then, yer look reet whacked," Sally continued after blowing her nose a few times on her apron. "So just close yer eyes, an' I'll tell yer a yarn. A bit of a nap before yer eat, eh?"

"Yes, we are tired," Helen managed to say.

"Aye, them's sleepy eyes if I'm a washerwoman," Sally said, sitting down on the floor next to them. "It's all reet now… all reet now. No lion, nothin' wrong now, eh?" Her voice got quieter and slower.

Out of the corner of her eye Anna saw first Helen's head droop then Connie's, but she fought to keep her eyes open. She couldn't explain why, but something was not quite right. She just sensed it. An echo of something, a whisper of a voice somewhere. *You must go. There is danger.* Just as she turned her head to see where the voice was coming from, a hand snaked around her and covered her mouth and nose with a strange, musty-smelling cloth. Her breathing was going funny. She could hear Connie's and Helen's voices… but where were they? And there was laughing coming from somewhere…

Then another sound, a bit like groaning, far away, getting quieter. She was sinking.

Darkness spread over her eyes like two doors closing together. She was falling, plunging into nothing.

# Chapter Seven

Anna was dreaming. She was in a tunnel travelling quickly towards a light that seemed to be growing. A familiar voice was speaking to her, but it seemed to be coming from a lion, who had appeared from nowhere. "Anna, wake up," it was saying, shaking her arm with its paws.

"Anna, wake up!" The voice had changed. This time it was Helen who was speaking. "Anna, wake up, oh, do wake up!"

Yes, she must wake up. She would be late for school. She opened her eyes and looked around her. This wasn't her bedroom! Where was she?

She tried to speak, but her mouth ached. Strange – she couldn't remember going to the dentist. Then it all came back to her in a rush.

"Thank goodness you're alive. It's taken so long for you to wake up," Helen cried, throwing her arms around her sister.

"I'm alright, it's just my mouth… but where is Connie?"

"I'm here," Connie whispered from a little way off. Anna turned her head towards the voice. Her friend was there, rubbing her eyes, pale but alive.

"What happened?" Anna managed to ask.

Helen, who was the most awake, replied that she thought they had all been drugged. "I managed to bite the person's hand, so I didn't get as much of it as you and Connie did. I woke up first."

"But where are we?" Anna asked, gazing all around her.

"In some sort of wagon, I think that's what you call it," Helen replied. "It's on wheels. I had a quick look outside before you both woke up."

Just then Connie let out a loud cry, and Helen rushed to her side. Anna tried to get up, but a wave of dizziness hit her and she sat down again.

"Are you ill?" Helen asked.

Connie was frantically searching the pocket in her dress. "No! It's my mother's purse, it's gone… my mother's treasures. Everything gone. It was there on the barge, I remember looking for it because I was worried it might have fallen out when we were running away from the lion."

"Someone's stolen it," said Helen. "That's why we were drugged. Someone saw the necklace. I told you it was valuable."

"But who would steal it?" asked Anna, now feeling more awake.

Connie tried to speak, but her voice broke. With a huge sniff she tried again. "Someone… must have seen it or… or knew about it."

"Let me think," Anna said, trying hard to concentrate despite a dull headache. "It must have been someone who knew the necklace was there or saw it when you showed us the purse."

"But we have seen so many people today. It could be anyone."

"Also, it might not have been the necklace they were after," Helen added, not to be outdone by her twin sister. "Supposing it was… the feather. It could be from a rare bird in Africa. And maybe there are only a few of them left, and… yes, it's part of a headdress that the chief—"

"Helen, this is real, it's not a play." Anna's voice was unusually sharp.

"Don't be hard on her," said Connie, unsmiling. "She only wants to help."

An awkward silence was broken by the wagon door opening. They hadn't heard anyone coming. Connie hid behind Anna and Helen, and they held their breaths as a young woman carrying a wicker basket came in. "Oh, thank the good Lord you're all awake. Me name's Minnie, and there's no harm in me."

They didn't reply. Anna was relieved that Helen didn't blurt anything out. It was better they say nothing at all.

"When we found you all dumped like you were, well, us was worried for your lives. If it wasn't for Bill – that's the dog – going off like he did, you might've all perished with the cold. That dog can sniff out anything not right."

The girls still didn't reply. Smiles and bright clothes may be masking something more sinister.

"Well, those be frightened faces," Minnie continued. "You needn't be. Us can give you a home here and a job. That is, Vinnie my husband will. He's not in charge – that's me – but he likes to sound important. Sorry, I'm rambling away. Vinnie says, oh Minnie you're a church bell, always dinging. Well, so it is – but watch this." Then, to the girls' surprise, Minnie turned a perfect triple cartwheel in front of them, followed by the splits and another cartwheel. This jaw-dropping display was completed with an elegant pose, followed by a low, deep curtsy. "Welcome to our world. Vinnie and Minnie's circus!"

"The circus! How wonderful! All those elephants and lions... oh—" Helen stopped suddenly, covering her mouth with her hand.

"Yes," said Minnie, chuckling a little. "That's where you are. This wagon is part of Minnie and Vinnie's travelling circus. Course, we're not travelling now, just parked up for the winter. But come the spring? What joy, on the road again."

Anna, not wanting Helen to say too much more, replied that they were very grateful for the offer of a job and home, but if Minnie didn't mind they would be off soon.

"Oh, if you're running away from something it's alright. Us give jobs to runaways. Us don't ask questions. Anyway, have a think. And here's me church bell dinging again when there's food for you to eat." Minnie opened the basket and took out three large chunks of bread and some cheese. She put them on a nearby table.

The girls backed away. Anna knew what the others were thinking. This time they were taking no risks.

"Hey, it's alright, it's not poisoned, but… well, Minnie said no questions, so looks as if Minnie will just have to show you all." She broke a chunk of bread in half then broke a bit off each end and ate it. Then, doing the same with the other two chunks, she ate them slowly and then ate some morsels from the middle. "There you are, still alive. So I reckon it's safe for you all to eat."

No one moved.

"We would rather not, because—" Anna had no time to finish her sentence, as Helen suddenly darted forwards, broke off a piece of bread and tucked into it hungrily. Anna and Connie had no time to stop her. Anna felt her throat go dry and her heart begin to race. "Helen," she cried, "spit it out!"

"No!" said Helen. "I believe her. Count to… twenty," she stuttered with her mouth full of bread. "And if I haven't fallen in a dead faint then I'm alright."

Silence.

"Just do it… oh… forget it." Helen swallowed it all down, smiling. "There you are. I feel fine. I'll count to twenty myself now. One… two…"

By twenty, nothing had happened.

Minnie grinned. "Not poisoned, see? Minnie wouldn't do that. Us wouldn't poison anybody. I might say us are hurt, but this has shown me just what jobs you can do, so I'm all cheered up. You're no-nonsense lasses. Eat now, and Minnie will go and get your costumes. Then us will see a sight to behold."

# Chapter Eight

"Goodness me, you gave me a fright," Anna said to Helen after Minnie had gone. "Don't do that again."

"But it was a brave thing for Helen to do," said Connie.

"I know," replied Helen, looking pleased with herself. "I'm starving. No more messing, let's eat."

Wasting no time, they tucked into the bread and cheese and soon felt much better with full stomachs. A little while later Minnie returned with some watered-down beer, which they drank gratefully.

"Now for costumes," said Minnie, reaching into her basket. "Stand up straight, and no talking about not joining us. Us have a good life, so yer all think on it." Going first to Connie, Minnie took out a beautiful deep gold dress with a pale gold bodice. A pale cream collar trimmed with lace gave the dress a look of elegance. Minnie held it against Connie. "There, look now, see how the colour matches your eyes."

Connie said nothing, and Anna wondered what she was thinking. Had Connie ever owned such a beautiful dress? Probably not.

Minnie beamed. "You will ride a horse as my African princess. Us will show you how to sit. Of course, you will wear a head dress, so no bother about your hair. You have the courage – I have seen that. You will hold your head high." She turned towards Anna and Helen. "You two will be servants to the princess. Walking on either side of the horse, you will roll hoops along and twirl and catch them. You'll learn quickly, I know. The audience will clap and cheer. They'll pay well to see you."

Reaching into her basket again, Minnie took out two dresses of the same size but different colours. The pale green dress she handed to Anna and the rich dark red one to Helen, and they stood up, holding the dresses against themselves. There was no doubt that both dresses were magnificent. "I thought so. Wonderful for the opening season—"

she folded the dresses carefully and placed them back in the basket, "—but for now it's school. You'll need lots of training, but you'll soon learn. So, what do you think? Have a talk, and us will come back later."

"So… what do we do?" asked Helen after she had left.

Connie opened her mouth to speak, but Anna put her hand on her shoulder. "Don't answer yet, Connie. Before you say anything, there's something you need to know about Helen and me. I think we should sit down."

Helen nodded. She knew what was coming next. The time had come for the complete truth. Would Connie believe their incredible story?

This wasn't going to be easy.

Anna slowly told Connie their tale. "This is honestly the truth, the whole truth, and nothing but the truth," she said as she finished. She knew that was what people said in court.

Silence fell. It was hard to know what Connie was thinking, as she was staring into space. After a few moments, she slowly turned her head and looked into Anna's eyes. "It is unbelievable. I'm not sure if I have taken it all in. My brain is still fuddled… but I believe you, because you have believed in me."

"Thank you." Anna suddenly felt emotional.

"We were worried about saying it earlier in case…" Helen paused, "…Anna, are you alright? You look like you've seen a ghost."

Anna didn't answer. She was beginning to feel strange again – something to do with the theft of the purse and the necklace. Little jigsaw pieces were moving around in her mind, trying to form a picture but then moving away. Moving… was something in the wrong place? Something she had seen or heard or…? Something important she should have recognised but missed somehow.

Her nose began to tickle with a sneeze, and she had no handkerchief. Quickly, to prevent coughing over everyone, she put her hand over her nose and mouth, catching the sneeze and then rubbing her hand on her dress. Suddenly a light came on in her brain. The jigsaw pieces arranged themselves into a picture. *That was it.* She jumped up. "Connie, Helen, I've got it! I know who stole the purse and the necklace."

"Who?" Helen cried.

"Yes, who?" asked Connie in a steadier voice.

Anna looked directly at her. "I can't tell you," she replied, feeling bad about it. "Connie, really, I can't, but it does mean we have to go back to

Keighley. I know it's hard not telling you all, but it might be dangerous and—"

"Go back? Go back there?" Helen blurted out. "You must be mad, someone has just tried to poison us! Anna, we can't."

"Connie, it is for you to decide, not us," Anna continued. "What do you want – stay in the circus and make your fortune, or look for the purse and the necklace? Or forget all of that and look for Maccle instead?"

Connie said nothing, pacing the floor in the corner of the wagon. There was a tense silence as they waited for her to make a decision. Connie mouthed some words, and Anna thought they might be the Bible verse from the purse. They watched her close her eyes and press her hands together. "Do you think she's praying?" whispered Helen to Anna.

"Hush, she will hear you," Anna said softly. "Promise you won't ask anything when she decides?"

Helen nodded.

After a few minutes, which seemed to go on forever, Connie stopped pacing and turned to them. "As I told you, I have no brothers and sisters. I do not think Mother would want me to join the circus.

She wanted me to have a home. If you want to go now, I will look for Maccle on my own."

"No," Helen cried. "We promised we would go with you, and we will."

"Yes. A promise is a promise," Anna agreed.

"Oh, I have never known such kindness from strangers. I want to go to Maccle to have a new home and someone to love me. But now I have found you both it feels like home here with you." She threw her arms round them both. Tears ran down each face and joined together, forming one single fountain as they drew closer, black and ginger hair blended in one big hug.

"Anna, are you absolutely sure you know who stole my mother's purse?" Connie asked.

"Yes, I am, but I will not say the name because we must keep safe. There might be spies anywhere. But the thief will not run away from Keighley, I know that."

"Then, in honour of my mother, whose purse was so precious to her, we will go back and find it. And hopefully find the person who stole it."

"I am glad," said Anna. "Yes, it might be dangerous, but we are better together."

There was no time for more words, as just then the door opened and Minnie stepped in. Over one arm she carried the costumes they had seen earlier. She peered closely at each face in turn. "Well, you all look as though you're sinking with the fever, red faces and damp hair."

"Oh, no," said Anna. "It's just that we have… just been talking. We are very grateful for your offer of work, but we need to go – to get back." It was a flurried speech, but it would have to do.

"That's all three of you, then?" Minnie asked.

"Yes," said Connie in a quiet but definite voice.

Minnie sighed. "Well, so it be then. It's a shame, mind. But if you change your minds anytime us will be waiting."

"Thank you," said Helen.

After Minnie left the wagon, Helen looked at Anna and spread her hands. "What now, then? You're in charge, sister."

"Look," said Anna, "I'm not the boss, and if I do get bossy tell me. But I reckon you and me should stop looking like maids."

"Yes, definitely," Connie said. "I will tell you what to do. Fold the top bit of your apron down behind the bottom bit then tie it round your waist."

"Like this?"

"Right. Good. Now put your caps in your pockets." She waited, then, "Now do your hair in plaits. You can tie them with a bit of wool pulled from your shawl. It's just as well you both look dirty, that helps."

"Well, will we do?" Anna asked after they'd followed Connie's instructions.

"Yes, you will, but always wrap your shawl around your head. Keep covered as much as you can."

"Thanks. Are we all ready?" Helen asked, looking first at one then the other.

"Yes," replied Anna. "A plan came to me while we were getting changed. We earn our way back to Keighley, doing little jobs on the way. But like Connie said, we must not stay long in case we're put in the workhouse."

"It is a good plan," Connie said, kissing the twins' cheeks. "God keep us safe."

# Chapter Nine

"So, which way do we go then?" Helen asked once they'd climbed out of the wagon. "Let's not stand around too long; it's freezing."

All three of them pulled their shawls tighter round their heads and shoulders as they took in their surroundings. To their surprise, they were not in a town, but on a country road bordered by fields and hedges. The only thing in sight was the circus with all its wagons and horses.

"The wagon must have brought us a long way when we were drugged," Anna said. "Let's try that way – it looks like it might lead to a town."

They began to walk. They passed all the wagons and trudged down the road, one weary step at a time. The road seemed to go on forever. It seemed like a road to nowhere. No buildings, nothing to guide them. They had no idea where they were going. Anna knew that, and she felt bad; it had been her idea. Surely there would be something soon – a farm, a village or maybe, if they were fortunate, a town?

Sometime later Connie stopped. "I can't go on, I don't feel right." Without any warning she fell to the ground, her body twitching in jerky movements. Helen and Anna dropped to the ground next to her, frantically calling her name over and over again. After a few moments, Connie stopped shaking and became very still, her eyes shut tight.

"She's dead, I know it," cried Helen.

"Stop panicking!" Anna replied, her voice trembling a little. "She's not. Look, her chest is going up and down."

Helen looked. It was. "What do we do—"

"Hush," interrupted Anna. "I can hear something in the distance. Listen."

Sure enough there was something approaching. Horses' hooves.

Anna and Helen turned their heads just in time to see a horse and carriage come into view, driven by a man in a smart green uniform.

This was their chance. They ran into the road and waved. The horse whinnied, raised its front legs and came to a sudden stop. The man in the green uniform jumped down. "What the dickens were you playing at? Never run in front of a horse like that. You could have had us all killed."

"What is it, Stoats?" The carriage door opened, and a woman dressed in fine clothes leaned out.

"Pardon, my lady, but these foolish children ran out and startled the horse. I do hope your ladyship is not hurt."

"I am uninjured, Stoats, but help me down. I must see these children."

"Yes, my lady."

Anna and Helen, crouching back at the side of the road with Connie, watched as the woman was helped out of the carriage. Gathering her long dress up to avoid some mud, she walked over to them. "Now, what is this about?"

"Sorry, your ladyship, but our friend here is incapacitated and likely to die. She was shaking and twitching and everything." Helen pronounced each word slowly and respectfully, then scrambled to her feet and dropped a deep curtsy.

Anna saw a tiny smile form on the woman's face and gave Helen a slight nudge in the ribs.

"Well, let me see," said the woman kindly. Kneeling down, she put one ear to Connie's face, then stood up, brushing off her skirts. "Your friend is breathing normally. It might be some sort of faint, but I don't know for sure. Stoats, carry this young lady to the carriage and lay her gently on the seat. You two, follow us. We will return to Wishwell Hall. This child needs a doctor."

"Yes, my lady."

It was clear to both Anna and Helen that Stoats was not happy about the idea. Glaring at them both, he bent down and lifted Connie rather roughly.

"Careful, Stoats! She's a child, not a sack of potatoes."

"Pardon, my lady."

The woman pointed into the carriage. "Lay her here. Now then, one of you sit next to your friend and the other next to me."

As the carriage moved off, Anna leaned forward to look out of the window. There was nothing she recognised, just fields and trees. Were they any nearer to Keighley? She had no idea. It was right to get Connie help, but supposing Wishwell Hall wasn't near anything? How were they going to get back on track again? She had not reckoned on this, not at all.

A minute or two later Connie opened her eyes. She did not move but looked around, a blank expression on her face.

"It's alright, my dear," the lady said. "You were taken ill. I am Lady Louisa. You are in my carriage. Your friends are here too. I'm taking you to my home, Wishwell Hall. A doctor will attend you there, so just close your eyes now."

Connie looked first at Anna and then at Helen. Both nodded in agreement, so Connie obeyed and closed her eyes.

No one spoke after that.

It was the first time the twins had sat in comfort since their arrival in the past. It was good to be out of the wind. The rhythmic clip-clop sound of both horses' hooves on the road was soothing. They found themselves getting sleepy and closed their eyes. Without them knowing anything about it, the carriage continued its journey.

It only seemed a few minutes later when the carriage stopped, jolting the three children awake. A few seconds later Stoats appeared at the door. "Thank you, Stoats. Fetch Renton for me," Lady Louisa said.

"Yes, my lady." He turned and walked away.

Turning to Anna and Helen, Lady Louisa said, "Here we are. Renton, my footman, will come and carry the young lady upstairs to Miss Caroline's old playroom. Mrs Staley, my housekeeper, will show you your room, which is on the same floor."

Gazing out of the carriage door, neither twin could speak. This house was a mansion! Very grand, with too many windows to count. Light streamed out of some of them, cheering a wintry day. Other windows were empty of light. Here was a house that welcomed you yet made you feel solemn too.

"Do not be frightened," Lady Louisa continued, as though reading their thoughts. "You will be well looked after."

Anna managed a slightly awed 'thank you'. Helen made a better attempt by saying, "Thank you, your ladyship," in her best polite voice only used for vicars and teachers.

Just then a young man in a jacket with very shiny buttons walked up to them. "You asked for me, your ladyship?"

"Yes, Renton. I want you to carry the young lady here to Miss Caroline's old room. We will follow you upstairs."

The lad helped Lady Louisa and the girls out of the carriage then reached in and lifted a quiet, unprotesting Connie carefully, and set off towards the house. It was early dusk now. The day was dying. Somewhere in the distance a solitary owl hooted – whoo, whoo – sounding just like a lost child wailing for its mother.

# Chapter Ten

They were met in a large hall by the housekeeper, Mrs Staley, who neither walked nor ran but seemed to skim over the polished floor towards them, straightening her cap at the same time. She came to a sudden halt and did a jerky curtsy. "I am sorry, my lady. We – I did not expect you back so soon."

"Do not stress yourself. Buying hats can wait. On the road we came across these children who need our help, so we came back. One of them is sick. Send for Doctor Hart, will you?"

A maid was summoned and given orders to fetch the doctor.

Up until then the housekeeper had kept her eyes only on her mistress. She now cast a sideways glance at the three of them, and Anna thought for a moment she saw her lip curl, but it was replaced quickly with a rather forced smile. Lady Louisa nodded to Renton, who made for the stairs with Connie. "Don't jolt the child, or bump her head," Lady Louisa instructed as she followed, with Mrs Staley, Anna and Helen close on her heels.

Halfway up the stairs, Helen began to slow down. Anna, sensing something was bothering her sister, slowed her pace, raising her eyebrows in a question. "You don't think it's a trap, do you?" Helen whispered. "I mean… her poshness arriving like that?"

Anna frowned. "No, how would she know we would be there?"

"That Minnie circus woman could be in on it; she could've told her."

"How? They don't have phones."

Helen looked thoughtful. "No, suppose not – but what if we have been lured away only to die a horrible death in a dungeon under the floor?"

"What are you on about? It's not Henry VIII days!" Anna grinned. "But still… keep your eyes and ears peeled, I suppose."

"And you," Helen said. "We had better catch them up."

Two flights of stairs later, Renton stopped. "Put her in the bedroom next to mine," Lady Louisa said.

"Yes, my lady," Renton replied, a little breathless. Mrs Staley moved in front and, plucking a bunch of keys from her belt, opened the door.

Anna and Helen looked around at the room. It must at one time have been a nursery. At one end there were several ancient-looking children's toys, including a rocking horse and a doll's house. Renton laid Connie down on the bed, and Lady Louisa covered her with a thick, beautifully embroidered gold-and-red bedspread. "There now, rest, my dear," she said, straightening the bedspread a little. She turned to the housekeeper, who was lingering in the doorway. "Mrs Staley, show these two to the room that was Lady Dorothy's, and then return. I will need you to be here when the doctor comes."

"Yes, my lady," Mrs Staley said, beckoning to Anna and Helen to follow and then leading them a little way down the corridor. "Right, here you are," she said, unlocking a door and pushing it open then turning quickly away and striding off up the hallway.

"She's a bundle of joy," Helen muttered.

"Reminds me of Nurse Barton," Anna said, going to the window and looking out at the evening sky.

Helen screwed up her face, remembering the humiliation of the school nurse rummaging through her hair for nits. Shaking her head to get rid of the memory, she gazed around the room. "Brilliant and beautiful," she said, taking in the pale pink curtains with matching bed cover, the long, cushioned window seat, the pale cream furniture, and many Victorian things she couldn't name. "And look, there's another door." She walked over and peered in. "Anna! It's another bedroom," she called out. "This is heaven. One each!"

No reply.

"Anna, you're not listening."

"I heard you," Anna replied, a little irritated. "That's nice, but I'm thinking about Connie. Supposing she is very ill? Supposing she... well..."

"You don't mean... *dies*? It would be awful."

"Yes," Anna replied. "It would. And then what—"

"You mean, what do we do then?"

Anna said nothing. They slumped down on the soft bed and sat for a while, taking in their surroundings and talking about everything that had happened that day. Exhausted, they sank back against the pillows and felt themselves dozing off…

A sudden knock on the door made them jump. Anna ran to open it, rubbing bleary eyes. How long had they been asleep? It was dark outside. An unsmiling maid stood there, staring at them both. She didn't speak for a moment, as though she was trying to find the right words. "S… sorry to disturb you, miss," she finally stuttered. "But her ladyship has told me to bring you both to the young lady what is ill."

Anna's stomach lurched. Had her worst fears already come true? She glanced at Helen, noticing she looked very pale. "Oh, no… Connie?" she gasped.

Following the maid along the corridor, Anna and Helen hurried to Connie's room. The maid tapped on the door and then edged it open, allowing them just enough space to squeeze through. Mrs Staley, who was standing a little way off, came forward and met them at the doorway. She frowned at the maid. "Raise your head and don't look so miserable," she said crossly. "You are an upstairs maid now."

The maid mumbled something about being sorry and, rabbit-like, she darted away.

"Sorry, my lady, still training her up," said Mrs Staley, standing back to allow Anna and Helen in.

Lady Louisa greeted them with a warm, "Here you are." Then, standing back to allow them to see Connie, she beckoned them across.

Standing by Connie's bed was a balding man. And there, sitting up in bed, was Connie, alive and smiling. Holding her hands out. Anna and Helen ran towards her, both trying to be the first one to give her a hug. Connie laughed. "I'm alright, really, I am. It was just because of tiredness. A few days in bed is all that is needed."

The man smiled. "Yes, that is correct, the young lady has spoken well."

"This is Doctor Hart, the Dellaway family doctor," Lady Louisa said. "My full name is Lady Louisa Dellaway."

Anna felt nervous. Doctors often made her feel like that. They always made her think of injections and pink medicine. She gave her sister a look.

"Oh, yes… thank you," said Helen, coming to her sister's rescue. "It's our special honour to meet you." The speech was accompanied with a little nod of the head and finished off with a wide smile. Helen looked pleased with herself.

Lady Louisa smiled too. "Well, as Shakespeare once said, all's well that ends well."

# Chapter Eleven

Back in their own room later, the twins sat together on Anna's bed. "Lady Louisa Dellaway, what a lovely name," Helen sighed.

"Yes, and that tea we had in Connie's room, crumpets and everything. I've eaten so much I'll burst."

"Me too. Did you see that look of amazement on Connie's face when Miss Misery Maid brought it in?"

Anna laughed. "Don't suppose Connie's ever had so much food at one time."

Helen nodded. "Yes, no wonder she fell asleep so quickly afterwards. So, now what?"

"Well, we need to find out where we are and how many miles it is to Keighley. I'm thinking not to ask Lady Louisa for help."

"But if we told her everything, then she can get that Stoats man to give us a lift."

"It's not like catching a bus, Helen. A carriage is seen by people. We have to get back in a way that no one sees."

"Oh, you mean the…" Helen trailed off, glancing around and lowering her voice. "You don't think there are… secret panels, or things where people can listen in to what we are saying, do you?"

Anna chuckled. "No, don't be daft. These thick walls could swallow the noise of an army all shouting together."

"Oh, that's scary. Suppose there were men outside with long spears waiting until we go out?"

"Give it a rest, Helen. Concentrate. Being here could be useful – a bed to sleep in, food to eat, no wandering from place to place trying to earn money. Flipping brilliant. We'll keep a look out, start to ask questions, find out things."

"Oh, absolutely, just what we need. And if breakfast is just as good as the tea we've just had—"

"You and your stomach," Anna interrupted. "Now, to start with, how about we have a chat with Miss Misery Maid in the morning?" She yawned. "Oh, blow it, can't think now. I need some sleep."

"Oh, yes, and me too, definitely," said Helen. "Just think of sleeping in a four-poster bed with curtains all around it. And I've just spotted some nighties on that chair for us to change into. How did they get there?"

"The maid must have put them there."

"Oh, yes, she must've brought them in when we were with Connie. I'm beginning to like Miss Misery Maid. Oh, the relief to be able to take this maid's uniform off and put something more comfortable on." She fetched the nightdresses and, holding one up against her body, she smiled. The hem almost touched the ground. "Look at that, perfect. Just like my own at home. How did Lady Louisa know they would be just the right size for us? Oh, flipping heck, you don't think she's a witch, do you?"

"Will you stop imagining stuff? She's not a witch. I expect they have some clothes for when relatives visit."

Helen sighed. "You can be so boring at times, but as I'm in a good mood, I forgive you. Right, I'm going to get into mine—" She reached to untie her apron.

Suddenly Anna jumped up and grabbed her arm. "Stop! No, don't do anymore. Seeing you doing that made me remember how we found the trunk and put the maid uniforms on."

"So?"

"Think! If we took them off, we might end up at Grandma's kitchen back in our own time."

"Oh… I was just about to take my apron off. But what do we do? I can't sleep in these clothes."

Anna sat down. "Let me think…" She mused a while. "Got it. Supposing we just undo our aprons, but we hold onto them and see what happens? If we feel a bit funny then we fasten them again."

"Right, and we do it together," said Helen.

"Yes. I will count *one, two, three,* and we'll put our arms around our backs, and then I'll say *go*. Come on, let's stand together. Now. One, two, three… go!"

They both undid their apron strings.

Nothing happened.

"I feel alright, do you?" Anna asked.

"Yes," Helen replied, "and we are still here."

"Right then, now we take our aprons off."

Again, nothing happened.

"Right, this time we grab our nighties, stick them under our arms, and when we take our dresses off we immediately put the nighties on."

They did so and as quickly as they possibly could.

Success! They had taken their maid uniforms off – and they were still in Victorian times.

"Thank goodness for that," Helen said, clapping her hands together. "Guess it just wasn't the right time. We have to stay here, and that's not imagination."

"Sorry, and yes, you're right. We are here for a reason; we must keep going. And we must hang onto these maid clothes. I reckon they will be our way back."

"Right. Let's put them under our pillows so they won't get lost."

"Good idea," Anna replied, yawning again. "And now I am so sleepy I will fall down in a minute."

Helen laughed. "Four-poster bed, oh joy! See you in the morning."

She skipped away through the connecting door. Anna managed to turn off the gaslight after a few tries and felt her way back to her bed. It was very dark. She wasn't usually afraid of the dark, but she got into bed as quickly as she could and pulled the blankets as near to her chin as possible. It was so very quiet and just a bit scary.

But not for long, as the next thing she was aware of was Helen, jumping on her bed. "Wake up, you! It was a brilliant sleep, it's morning, and I'm famished."

# Chapter Twelve

Anna opened her eyes, startled. "Did you have to wake me up like that? You are always thinking of your stomach."

"Do you think breakfast will be as good as that tea we had?"

Anna sighed. It was no use. Helen had said the same thing last night – she always had food on her mind. Anna sat up, turned back the blankets, and got out of bed. "Right then, before anything else," she said, reaching under her pillow for her shawl and wrapping it around her, "We must go to Connie and see how she is."

"Oh, sorry… yes. I mean—"

"And don't overdo it, come on."

Anna didn't wait for an answer as she padded to the door with Helen following, her face a little pink. Anna knocked on Connie's door then, opening it a little, she peered in. Connie was sitting up in bed with a new shawl around her shoulders. "Come in," she called out.

"Oh, look at you," cried Helen, happy to see Connie looking so well. "You look like a princess in that shawl."

"The maid brought it. She said that Lady Louisa had told her to make sure I was cosy and warm. I will be having my breakfast in bed too."

"You look so much better," Anna said. "I guess it was the tea and the sleep."

"Yes, I needed it. I have never been so comfortable. Come and sit next to me."

Anna and Helen sat down on each side of her. "Well, it's a new day," Anna began. "I hope we find out some useful stuff—"

Just then there was a tap on the door and the maid came in.

"Oh, good," Anna whispered. "Just the right person – and at the right time too."

Anna and Helen moved aside, and the maid came forward carrying a tray laden with a steaming hot bowl of porridge, bread and butter, and a glass of milk. "Here's your breakfast, miss. Cook was told to make sure you have it fresh from t'kitchen. An' can I say, miss, you are looking ever so better. Word in the kitchen was that it were the typhoid, and us would all die."

"Thank you," said Connie, smiling. "And no, it is not the typhoid. I have seen it kill people in a day."

"Aye, it can, but best not to think on it," replied the maid with a slight shiver.

Connie propped herself up against her pillows, and the maid put the tray down in front of her. "Madam said the other two young misses are to have their breakfast downstairs in the dining room when them are ready. I have put water and towels an' some of Miss Flora's cast-off dresses in your room, as madam said."

"Oh, lovely. I mean, thank your mistress most kindly," replied Helen, trying her best to sound grand.

The maid turned to go. "Oh, stay a minute," said Anna quickly. "Can you tell us a bit about the house? I mean… Lady Louisa has been so kind to us."

"Oh, that she is, miss, kind to kiddies an' animals. No one round these parts is kind as madam is. The house belongs to madam. There is just her ladyship and her daughter, Miss Flora. The master, Lord Edgar Dellaway, died last year. He were a good master."

"Oh yes – Lord Edgar Dellaway, master of Wishwell Hall in…?"

"Yorkshire, miss."

Anna bit her lip to stop a laugh from coming.

"Oh, I get it now. Wishwell Hall is in't moors. Next village is Yatly, where I was born. But I must go, miss, as Mrs Staley will stop some of me wages if I idle."

"Well, that didn't tell us much," Anna said after the maid had gone. "Connie, have you heard of Yatly?"

Connie, spooning porridge into her mouth, just shook her head. She laid her spoon down. "I think you should have your breakfast now. You might get a chance to ask Lady Louisa yourself."

"Good idea," said Helen, darting to the door. "Then we can come back and make a plan. Glad you're better," she called out over her shoulder.

Anna followed behind her sister. Turning at the door to look at Connie, she mouthed the word 'famished' with a grin. Connie laughed and waved them away.

They returned to their own room to wash and dress. "Ready?" Anna asked a few minutes later.

"We certainly look like two posh Victorians now," replied Helen. "Lovely dresses. Now to find the dining room."

As they made their way downstairs, the smell of food lured them along a corridor. There were several doors, but which one led to the dining room? Pausing at one door then another, they hesitated to open any in case it was the wrong one. Fortunately, as they were wondering what to do next, a nearby door opened and the housekeeper came out. Seeing them standing there she ushered them in, her face blank and unsmiling as she pushed past them.

What they saw in the room made them gape in wonder. On a large oak table in the centre was a huge selection of food. It was nothing like the cereal and toast breakfast they had at home. Sausages, bacon, and eggs cuddled together on a large platter, cold meats on another. Bread rolls lay next to pots of jam. There was fish too, and porridge, and tea and coffee. This was a feast to behold.

"Come on in," Lady Louisa said, beckoning to them. "It's for eating, not staring at. And this is my daughter, Miss Flora. She has just returned from staying a few days with a friend."

"Oh, yes. Thank you... no, I mean, we are pleased to meet you," said Helen, doing a deep curtsy but then losing her balance and tripping over.

Miss Flora went to help Helen up, colliding with Anna who was also rushing to her side. Anna drew back a little, her face warm. "Do not mind," said Miss Flora. "I do not think your ... um..."

"Sister," replied Anna. "We are twins. Anna and Helen Price."

"Twins, how wonderful! I am Miss Flora. And look, your sister is fine now, and I think is in need of breakfast!"

Helen didn't try any more curtsies or grand speeches. She drew out a chair and sat down, Anna beside her. Miss Flora spread some jam on her roll. "Help yourself," she said, gesturing at the food and smiling.

The next few minutes were spent tucking into the best breakfast they'd had in their lives. The food was so good they completely forgot to ask about Yatly.

Lady Louisa left the room while they were still eating with instructions to her daughter to look after her new friends. All was now quiet. Anna noticed that Miss Flora was fiddling with a button on the front of her dress.

When they had finished the maid came in to clear everything away, and the moment she left, Miss Flora scraped her chair back and hurried round the table to sit with the twins. "We are alone now," she whispered. "Move your chairs closer. I must tell someone... can I trust you?"

Anna and Helen nodded together.

Miss Flora looked from one twin to the other. "I am in great danger. My Aunt Dorothy is trying to get rid of me."

"What?" said Helen.

"Why?" said Anna at the same time.

Miss Flora sighed. "As to what, I know it sounds unbelievable. As to why, I will tell you. I am eleven and an only child. I had an older sister, Miss Caroline, but she died of the pox two years ago. My father died in a riding accident last year. Mother said she would never marry again, so there will be no more children. That made her sad. This is why she takes pity on children like... erm..."

"Us?" Helen suggested.

"Well, yes, but I didn't mean—"

"That's alright," said Anna. "But maybe we should tell you our story before you go on. It's important if you want us to keep a secret."

"Oh, yes, I hadn't thought of that."

"So…" she began, and went on to tell the whole story apart from the bit about coming from a different time. She thought it better to leave that out.

Flora nodded. "I have heard of mills and other bad places. My governess says I must not ask too much about them. You are good girls, and Connie must be too. But maybe it would be best to go somewhere else to talk, just in case anyone comes in?"

"Definitely," said Helen, sounding rather relieved. "Where can we go?"

"We could go for a walk in the grounds to get warm and then go into the summer house?"

"Oh, absolutely," said Helen in an over-enthusiastic voice.

"But we really must go and see Connie now," Anna said.

"Of course. I will meet you in the hall in one hour." Flora left quickly, waving from the doorway.

"So, sister, was she for real?" Helen asked once they were alone. "She looked scared to death."

"Yes, but I don't know. I just can't believe that… it just sounds…"

"I know, me too. Is it a game or a play she does with everyone who comes here? It's like that 'whodunnit' play Mother was once in. It was supposed to be scary but wasn't." Helen did a pretend scream.

"That one when a bit of scenery fell over onto the stage?" Anna laughed at the memory of two startled actors jumping out of the way of collapsing cardboard trees.

Helen chuckled. "Oh, just think – we could call it 'Murder at Wishwell Hall: Death of the Upstairs Maid'. It was the cook in the pantry with the rolling pin."

Anna stopped laughing. "But… just suppose it *is* true. If it is, does it mean Miss Flora is in danger? And if so, will she ask us to help her?"

"If she is telling the truth, we have to talk to Connie right now."

"Yes, you're right. Let's go."

As they left, Helen stopped, gazing around the room. "What are you doing?" Anna demanded.

"I am making a food memory of my breakfast."

Anna sighed. "Oh, for goodness' sake, stop it. Come on, Connie will think we've run away."

"Alright, Miss Bossy."

# Chapter Thirteen

"That's all of it. What do you think?" Anna had just finished telling Connie all about meeting Miss Flora and what she had said. She was perched on one side of the bed, Helen on the other.

"How did she look?" Connie asked.

"How do you mean?" Anna said. "She had a nice blue dress on."

"No – her face. How did it look to you—"

"Oh, I know how it looked," interrupted Helen. "Her face went red all over, and her eyes went really big and starey. Also, she kept rubbing her hands in her hair."

"I have seen people look like that at the mill when they were frightened. Did she talk in a rush?"

"Yes, she did a bit, and she whispered a lot too," Anna said.

"She is telling the truth," Connie said, looking serious.

"Oh," Helen replied, lowering her head. "I got it wrong then."

"Don't feel bad about it. You didn't know. Go to the summer house. Listen to her. Then come back here – all three of you."

"We said we'd meet in an hour," Anna said. "A bit of it has already gone."

"Then stay here and talk to me until it's time to go. Tell me about your past lives."

The twins settled down to tell stories and memories of birthdays they had enjoyed, and Connie listened eagerly, sometimes smiling, sometimes sad. "I would like a life like yours. I very much hope… maybe one day." She sighed, lowering her head.

"We hope so too." Anna could feel her eyes going misty.

Helen reached out to squeeze Connie's arm.

They stayed there in companiable silence for a while, laying their heads back and closing their eyes. The noise of the clock chiming in the hall brought them back to the real world. "Time to go," Anna said, getting up off the bed.

"We won't be long," Helen said.

"It's alright. After all, I'm going nowhere," said Connie, chuckling to herself as the twins made their way to the door.

They left the room and went down the stairs to the hall, where Miss Flora was already waiting. There was no one else about. "Thank you for coming. I will show you around the house first. After that I will show you the outside buildings. It will look more natural."

The twins nodded and gave their best smile, trying to look as if they were in for a real treat. Miss Flora smiled back as she began to lead them on a historical tour of the house. As they passed the footman on the stairs, Anna saw Helen go pink and grinned to herself. Well, he was good-looking.

Outside the house there was more history to be discovered in the grounds. Flora led them through the gardens and down a long, winding path past a wishing well in front of a high wall. "Oh, how lovely!" Helen said, rushing towards the well.

"It's been there years," said Miss Flora. "That's why the house is called Wishwell Hall. No one visits it now. As you can see, lots of stones are loose. And the chain that pulls the water up is broken. Better not go too near it."

Helen stepped back and, casting a fond look at the well, caught up with the others as they continued along the path. They arrived at a pretty summer house a few minutes later, and Miss Flora pushed open the door. It was a relief to get out of the cold.

"That was very good," said Anna. "You know a lot of things about the house."

"My governess made me learn the history of it. But that is nothing. I have brought you here to tell you about the accidents."

"Accidents?" echoed Anna.

"Yes… to me."

"What sort of accidents?"

"They all happened over Christmas when Aunt Dorothy came. First a looking glass over the fireplace in the front parlour fell down when I was walking past, and it just missed me. The shock made me jump. I nearly fell into the fire. Aunt Dorothy was sitting nearby and came over supposedly to help, but I swear I felt her push me towards the fire. But just then Mama came in, and Aunt Dorothy pulled me to safety."

"That's awful," Helen cried. "You could have fallen into the fire and... oh, you could have been..."

"Yes, I know. That was just the first. Then there was the bedtime milk Aunt Dorothy brought me one night. She said she'd taken it from the maid. I took two mouthfuls but then stopped because it didn't taste right. I... oh! I have just seen Stoats. I don't know if he is coming this way... but look as though you are admiring the view."

Anna and Helen turned to look out of the window. Miss Flora pointed to a large majestic looking garden plant with dark purplish-red crinkly leaves. They bent down and peered at it with forced delight as they saw Stoats pass by out of the corner of their eyes. When he was gone, they straightened up.

"Best to be careful," said Miss Flora. "Right, where was I? Oh, yes – the drink. I pretended to be very sleepy. I closed my eyes and heard my aunt go out, then I made myself be sick out of the bedroom window. I reckon if something had happened the maid would have been blamed for it."

"Just as well it didn't," said Anna.

"Yes. Then there was the stairs. I slipped halfway down one morning. It was alright, though, because the footman was on his way up. He caught me before I fell all the way."

"Oh, how lovely," Helen sighed. "I mean… it must have been heavenly he was there."

"Yes, he was heaven-sent. At breakfast I told Mama. She said it might have been a bit of polish not rubbed in properly. Aunt Dorothy said something about the maid not doing her job right. Then, when she passed me the basket of bread, I noticed bits of yellow under her thumbnail."

"Yellow polish," said Anna.

"Yes, I felt sure it was. She went home that same day, said she was missing her dogs. Nothing else happened after that. But she is coming back today for New Year. She will be here for afternoon tea."

"Then you might be in danger again?"

"Yes."

"But why does she want to get rid of you?" Helen asked, jumping from one foot to another to keep warm.

"I will tell you why. Then we will go; it is getting cold. Now that my father and sister are dead, I will inherit the house when I am twenty-one. If I die and Mama too, the house goes to Aunt Dorothy as there is no one else left in the family."

"So, all she has to do is get rid of you both in turn." Helen hugged her arms around her chest.

"Yes. I think the idea came to her after Papa and Caroline died."

Anna saw tears forming in Miss Flora's eyes and one or two spilling down her face. "Then your aunt has to be stopped," she said quickly. "But let's think of a plan in Connie's room. It's freezing in here."

Miss Flora wiped her eyes with a lace handkerchief. "Yes, your friend sounds kind."

As they left the summer house and hurried back to Wishwell Hall, a single crow cawed its tuneless notes.

In Connie's room, Anna introduced Miss Flora to Connie, and they sat down next to her bed. Miss Flora told Connie everything she had just told Anna and Helen. Silence fell as Connie took in her words, and they all mused on what on earth they could do about it.

"I've got it." A smile grew on Helen's face. "Come a bit closer, and I will tell you."

A few minutes later, and with just a few alterations, everyone agreed to the plan. "That was a good bit of thinking," Anna said, smiling at her sister.

Helen grinned back. "See, I can be sensible."

"But we must be very careful. It's risky," Anna said, looking intently at Miss Flora.

Miss Flora stood up. "If it goes wrong, you mean?"

"Yes."

"It has to be done, for the sake of the family and the Dellaway name. I will do it. Tomorrow, then, but now I must go. Mama will be looking for me. She will want me to go riding with her."

"Now that is courage," Connie said after Miss Flora had gone.

"Yes," Anna replied.

"It would be best for you two to go now," said Connie. "The maid will be here soon to see to me. Spend the day doing ordinary things, but keep a look out. I will say a prayer for you all."

Anna and Helen spent some time outside, making up running-around games; it was a good way of keeping warm. Later, they went to their room and played 'silly hide and seek', hiding an object in the room with the other one searching for it while blindfolded. It was a bit boring, but it passed the time.

Eventually, to Helen's delight, it was lunch time. Lady Louisa and Miss Flora were back from their riding trip. It was nice to see them so happy together. Miss Flora did not speak to them at all during lunch, but after Lady Louisa left the room she came over. "Sorry, but I can't take any more risks. Meet me back in the summer house in a few minutes."

"Has something happened?" Anna asked.

"Tell you later." She turned and rushed out of the room.

In the summer house a while later, she smiled thinly at them. "Thanks for coming."

"Problems?" Anna asked.

"Just one. Mama wants me to take singing lessons with my aunt when she arrives. I forgot to tell you; she is an opera singer. Mama wants me to start tomorrow morning."

"Oh, bother."

"I know Aunt Dorothy will say yes. She is always going on about the joys of singing."

"Where will you be?" Helen said.

"In the music room, there's a piano in there. There is a harp too, which Mama plays, and some other instruments."

"What are the windows like?" Anna asked.

Miss Flora knitted her brows. "The windows? Oh... long, with thick light brown curtains that fall to the floor. Why do you want to know about the windows?"

"Perfect. It's so we can hide behind them and listen in."

"But she won't try anything there – it would make her the obvious guilty one, without anyone else around."

"Best to be sure, though," said Anna. "Yes, stick to what I've said. Show us the music room when we go in. Tell your aunt you want to start the lesson at ten o'clock, so we can already be hidden when you come in."

"Are you sure?"

"Yes. Then after a few minutes of singing, say you have a headache and want some fresh air. Start walking to where we planned, and we will get there by the way you told us about."

"It's a bit riskier, but if you are really sure… then yes."

"Yes, we are," Anna replied, looking at Helen who nodded her head.

They discussed the finer details of the plan, which they repeated just to make sure. "Are we happy with it all?" Anna asked.

"Yes," said Helen and Miss Flora together.

Miss Flora held her hands out to them. "Anna, Helen, I can only say thank you for believing in me. I am so grateful for everything. I will see that you are rewarded."

"Never mind rewards, just show us the music room," Anna said.

Miss Flora was true to her word. After showing Anna and Helen the music room, she left, telling them she would go to the library and spend the time reading until afternoon tea. Anna and Helen made their way to Connie's room and told her about everything that had happened.

Connie frowned. "Hmm. This might be more difficult now. When you hide, you will have to stand very still. Do you think you can do it?"

"We promised. We can't go back on it. So now we wait for the wicked aunt to arrive," said Anna.

"Then stay here with me until teatime."

"Do you know a game called 'I Spy'?" Helen asked.

"No... but you can show me."

\* \* \*

When Anna first saw Miss Flora's aunt at afternoon tea, she was completely surprised. Anna had expected her to be ugly or at least a bit plain, or sniffly or wearing glasses on the end of her noise. But Aunt Dorothy was beautiful, tall, and slim with glowing light brown hair and milky cream skin. Could this beautiful woman really be bad?

At least neither of them was asked many questions. Aunt Dorothy did most of the talking and mostly about herself, her opera concerts, her dogs, and the latest fashions in hats. Lady Louisa seemed happy to listen. Miss Flora sat in silence, her face a little pale.

Anna and Helen went back to their own room after tea and flung themselves onto Anna's bed. "Phew, glad that's over. I can breathe now," Helen said. "Didn't expect the wicked aunt to look like that!"

"No, she's more like a queen in a fairy story. But as Mother once said in a play, 'fair skin, dark heart'. Anyway, we mustn't think too much – just get through the rest of the day."

# Chapter Fourteen

The following morning after breakfast, a few minutes before ten, Anna and Helen made their way to the music room. As they passed the housekeeper on the way they said a polite "good morning" and were totally ignored. Helen stuck her tongue out at her retreating back.

"Stop it," Anna snapped. "This is serious."

"Sorry, miss," Helen replied, putting her tongue out again.

Anna ignored her. Helen, dawdling a few steps behind, started to hum. Anna turned, giving her a look. "Alright, I'm sorry… just nervous, that's all," Helen blurted out.

"Me too, come on."

They reached the door and stopped. "Hush. Don't make a sound," Anna whispered. "Someone could be in there."

"Wouldn't it be better if we just went in? I mean, if the witch aunt is there we could just say we're looking for a… er… book…? One we've just lost."

"It could work, but best to open it slowly."

Helen nodded and began to turn the doorknob a little bit at a time. After a few tense seconds it clicked. They waited. Silence.

"Try opening it a bit more at a time," Anna suggested.

Helen did so until the door was open enough to look inside. The room was empty.

"Phew, my heart was in my mouth," Anna breathed.

They searched around the room. The windows and curtains were just as Miss Flora had described. The piano was in the centre of the room, with a long piano stool that two people could sit on. There were several upright chairs. By the wall stood a large sofa.

"Best thing to do is hide behind the curtain at that window over there. Then we will be behind Miss Flora and the aunt," said Helen.

"Very good," Anna replied, looking impressed. "Right, let's take up our positions and hope it all goes to plan. No talking from now on."

Anna and Helen tiptoed to the window and hid behind one curtain each. Anna's heart began to beat faster. She didn't like not being able to see Helen; she depended on her sister more than she let on. As she waited, she grew more nervous. Things could go badly wrong. At least their first plan, though risky, was better. They had decided that Miss Flora was to ask Aunt Dorothy at breakfast to go with her to the wishing well. The idea was they would each wish that Lady Louisa would find a new love. Miss Flora was to lean over, giving her aunt the chance to push her in. Miss Flora knew of a piece of brick that was loose. If her aunt tried to push her, she would grab the brick then throw it over her aunt's head, hoping she would duck. Anna and Helen were to go to the same place by a different path where they wouldn't be seen and hide behind a bush. Then, just when Aunt Dorothy ducked, they would jump out and grab her arms from behind. Miss Flora would tie some string around Lady Dorothy's hands, then together they would march her back to the house.

Now, because of this unexpected change in their schedule, so much more depended on Lady Dorothy taking the bait. Anna could hardly breathe. Oh, how she wanted to take Helen's hand.

She did not have to wait long. Just then she heard the sound of the door being opened.

Footsteps clicked across the room. She could hear a swishing of a long dress on the floor, then the scraping of the piano stool being pulled out. The aunt; it had to be.

The door opened again. She counted the new footsteps, ten quick steps – good – and then ten little skips. Good. Miss Flora was acting the part of the happy niece. Now for the words they had agreed on. "I'm so happy, Aunt, that you are willing to give me singing lessons."

"Well, Flora, your mother asked me, and of course I agreed straight away. The Dellaway family has a tradition of fine, excellent singers."

"I so want to make the family proud."

"Well, to begin with you need to pronounce your vowels correctly. Copy me."

The next few minutes were filled with Aunt Dorothy and then Miss Flora singing the five vowels, accompanied by the piano. Anna was pleasantly surprised that Miss Flora could sing so well.

"Yes, a good start, Flora dear. You certainly have potential. It means practice, though, and dedication, also a great deal of hard work."

"Yes, Aunt, but could I be excused from any more singing this morning? I find now I have a headache."

"Oh, of course, dear. Maybe a lie down will do you good?"

"Oh no, I… I mean… maybe not. I think a walk would help. Oh, I know – to the wishing well. I do have a secret wish to make."

"Ah, a wish. I used to make some, but… things changed. But wrap up well, it's cold today. How about we continue tomorrow?"

"Yes, thank you, Aunt."

Anna listened for Miss Flora's footsteps and the little cough she would give as she got to the door. Sure enough, it came. Anna waited for the aunt to go, but she didn't. Anna was frustrated. It meant they had to stay hidden.

Suddenly, Aunt Dorothy began to sing. It was a stupid, sloppy, grown-up love song. She was well away, the music rising higher, the notes clear. Then, unexpectedly, she missed a high note. She tried again, but her voice cracked and, with a tremendous thump, she slammed the piano lid down, the sound echoing through the room then dying away, leaving an empty silence.

Was she still there? Anna did not know. She dared not peek. The plan had to work!

After a few tense moments, Anna heard a knock on the door. Someone was coming in quickly. Light footsteps… not Miss Flora, surely?

"Excuse me, Lady Dorothy." To Anna's relief, it was the maid. "Sorry to disturb you, but the mistress has just seen Miss Flora outside and wondered what the matter was, is I mean."

"Oh, of course, yes… I will go after her."

"Thank you, my lady."

Anna heard them both leave. *Good*, she thought, *the plan is going to work after all*. She dared a quick peek around the curtain just to make sure they had gone. They had; the room was empty.

"Helen," she whispered, pulling the curtain away, "are you alright? It's safe to come out now."

Mole-like, Helen stuck her head out from behind her curtain. She looked pale and frightened. "That was awful, I didn't dare breathe."

"I know! We need to check the aunt has really gone." They turned and looked out of the window.

"There she goes, Lady Dorothy the cat." Helen pointed to where Lady Dorothy was striding along the path beneath.

"Right. We need to go... and no messing this time."

# Chapter Fifteen

Sprinting away from the house, Anna and Helen made their way to the agreed hiding place. It was hard to run after standing still for so long; their bodies ached, but there was no tine to lose.

Miss Flora had told them exactly where to go. This route was longer than the path they had taken when they had first seen the wishing well. It wasn't a path, really, only a rough way around some trees and bushes. Miss Flora had described little landmarks along the way and the bush where they could hide. She had said the bush was shaped like an umbrella with thick branches. It was perfect, they had been told, with a good view of the wishing well.

As they ran they spotted each landmark, one by one. Helen began to slow down, panting. "Must be close now, I'm shattered. I can't do much more."

"We have to. Can't be far." Putting her arm around her sister's waist, Anna helped her along. A minute or two later they both saw the bush and raced towards it in a final burst of energy.

"Alright?" Anna whispered as they crawled underneath the bush.

"I will be in a minute," Helen whispered back breathlessly.

"I'll take a look and see if I can see anything," Anna said, easing a branch a little way to one side. "Oh, thank goodness, Miss Flora is there by the well. I can just see the loose brick. We aren't too late. She's bending over it, as we agreed, but no sign of Lady Dorothy."

"You don't think she saw us, do you? That would mess things up."

"I hope not – but we did as we were told. Those trees we passed were very close together – oh… hush, I think I heard something."

They both crouched there, very still. Anna saw Miss Flora turn her head. She must have heard the same thing. Then a smiling Aunt Dorothy came into view, carrying something in her hand. "She's coming."

Helen edged her way closer to Anna. There was just enough space for her to see out.

They watched as Miss Flora turned round. "Oh, it's you, Aunt Dorothy! I thought I heard something. I was just making up rhyming wishes for the new year. I think Mother would like this one: 'Push the old year away and may a new love come to stay.' Oh, I see you have been picking flowers."

"Yes, my dear, and all for you. All of them." Lurching forward with one big stride, Aunt Dorothy pushed Miss Flora towards the wishing well and then, pinching Miss Flora's cheek with a finger and thumb, she started to force the flowers into her mouth.

"Poisoned flowers! Oh no," hissed Anna. "She's trying to poison Miss Flora! Come on, we need to stop her!"

Springing nimbly out of the bush, Anna and Helen raced towards Miss Flora who was now pushing her aunt in the stomach. The force of the push took Aunt Dorothy by surprise, and she nearly lost her balance. "You little vixen! You think you can push me over, do you? Well, two can play that game." Grabbing hold of Miss Flora's long hair,

Lady Dorothy yanked her head over. Miss Flora screamed.

Anna dashed to one side of Lady Dorothy and made a grab for the poisoned flowers. Helen, running to the other side, bit Lady Dorothy's arm, causing her to let go of Miss Flora's hair, yelping, "So! You have friends, do you? Street urchins come to the rescue? Come any nearer and I will push her down the well."

Anna and Helen stood still. A slow smile snaked its way across Lady Dorothy's lips.

Out of the corner of her eye Anna saw Miss Flora reach over the side of the wishing well. She guessed she was searching for the loose brick. Just then, Anna thought she heard footsteps. Was someone coming? She must keep Lady Dorothy from running away. "If anything happens to Miss Flora, you will have three witnesses, your ladyship." Anna spoke deliberately and slowly, trying not to sound nervous.

"Didn't they teach you to count at school? Oh, of course. Street urchins don't go to school." Aunt Dorothy, her voice rising in volume, ended with a mocking laugh. A number of crows squawked their ugly way through the sky, sounding like the human voice they had just heard.

"But I did," growled a voice. It was Stoats, running towards them from the direction of their hiding place, his large, muscular arms held out in front of him. Grabbing Lady Dorothy's arms, he tugged them behind her back and held them in a vice-like grip. It was so quick she had no time to get away.

Anna and Helen took the string from Miss Flora and tied Lady Dorothy's hands together, then her feet, despite the few kicks aimed at them. Lady Dorothy was no match against the muscular frame of Stoats. Years of driving the carriage and working in the garden had given him the strength of an ox. The criminal was well and truly caught.

A torrent of unladylike language spurted from Lady Dorothy's mouth but ended abruptly when they all saw two figures hurrying towards them. Lady Louisa and Connie. Miss Flora ran to her mother, falling into her arms. There was silence for a moment.

Then, facing up to her sister, Lady Louisa looked her directly in the eye. After a few tense seconds, she said, "Dorothy, why? What has my daughter ever done to you?"

"This morning was the last straw. My voice cracked on a high note. There is no future for me now, an opera singer who cannot manage the high notes. And no hope of inheriting Wishwell Hall either. You try living where I live, Moorfield House, only four bedrooms! You have three times as many."

"But Dorothy—"

"No. You listen to me. Then when *she*... your beloved daughter... flounced off for a walk, the floodgates opened. I had to get rid of her. I'd tried before, but now was my chance."

No one spoke or moved.

"After that would be a few months of grieving for appearances' sake. Then you, my dear sister? Another accident. I would play the part of the devastated sister. Then the hall would be mine."

Lady Louisa's face crumpled. "Dorothy... you are my little sister! We played together as children!"

"Oh, yes, but I could never be the elder, could I? I would always be the sister of Lady Louisa of Wishwell Hall. Why should *you* have it all?"

"But Dorothy, we could have shared Wishwell Hall together, grown old in the home we were brought up in."

"No. You would always be the mistress. Anyway—" she sighed, "—it's over now. At least give me the dignity of untying me. Let me walk back to the house as a lady should."

"Stoats... untie Lady Dorothy."

"Yes, your ladyship."

It was done quickly, and Lady Dorothy made no move to escape.

"Thank you, Stoats, and also for your loyalty to me," Lady Louisa said. Stoats gave a little bow.

It was a silent group that made their way back to the house. They were still a silent group when they arrived. Before they entered, Lady Louisa turned and spoke to them all. "Flora, dear, you must go and lie down. You children go to the dining room. I will ask Mrs Staley to send the maid with some tea. I will also send for the doctor."

The clock in the dining room ticked away the seconds and minutes as the children waited. They said little as they drank their tea. After what seemed a long time, the door opened and Lady Louisa came in. Her face looked pale, her eyes red and sore. "Come with me now to the parlour."

They followed her silently and sat together on a sofa opposite Lady Louisa.

"I don't know how to thank you enough. I could not believe it at first. When Connie told me what was happening, I thought it was... well, part of her illness. My sister has gone home. I could not bear her going to prison. She has done a bad thing, but she is still my sister and a lady." Lady Louisa stopped speaking to wipe away some tears with her handkerchief. A few silent seconds went by as she looked down at the floor. Then, raising her head, she began again. "Lady Dorothy has agreed to leave the country. I will not see her again. She has done a bad thing. The doctor will be here soon to attend my daughter. I will make sure he attends to all of you, too. It's been very distressing."

Looking first at Connie and then at Helen, Anna managed a shaky, "Thank you, your ladyship."

"I think you should go to your own rooms now. After the doctor has been I will order a light lunch for you to be served there if he permits."

Lady Louisa got up and wandered over to gaze at a family picture on the wall. She sighed. The three of them took the hint, rose to their feet and crept away, closing the door behind them. Not wanting to make any noise, they tiptoed together up the stairs.

"Phew," said Helen when they reached the top. "That was really hard. That Lady Dorothy fought like a tiger."

"Yes," said Connie. "I'm glad I fetched Lady Louisa. It seemed to be taking so long."

"Sorry, can't talk," Anna moaned, and suddenly rushed away, holding her stomach and calling out, "I'm going to be sick."

"I think I am, too," said Helen, going white.

"Go," Connie urged. "We can talk better later."

Helen raced after her sister to their own room. Neither of them ate any lunch that day.

Later in the afternoon, when the doctor came, he said that the bruises on their legs would all fade away. The sickness was understandable, and a good sleep was all that was needed.

And that is what they did, exhausted with the events of the morning.

* * *

"Helen, are you awake?" whispered Anna an hour or two later. Standing by her twin's bed, she gently stroked her arm.

"I am now. Did you have to wake me just then? I was trying on a blue gown, pure silk with a—"

"Sounds lovely, but what are we going to do next?"

"Have afternoon tea with buttery crumpets, fancy cakes, little sandwiches and… I'm starving. We had no lunch."

"You got better quick! But we can't stay here forever. We have to go back to Keighley and find the necklace. But oh, it's hard to go."

"I know," replied Helen with a big sigh. "I will miss it all."

"Yes, me too. Let's go and talk to Connie."

"And Miss Flora, if we can."

But before they could do that there was a knock on the door, and standing there looking pale with red tear-stained eyes was Miss Flora herself. "I have come to say thank you… but more than that, I've come to ask if you will stay. Mama and I want to give you both and Connie a home."

# Chapter Sixteen

For a few seconds neither Anna nor Helen spoke. Helen was the one to shatter it with a choked sob. Anna felt the same but tried to swallow hers. "I… we… oh, how do I say this? We must go… but…" Anna could say no more; the sob would not be swallowed and choked her words.

"But why? Mama will be your Mama too… and we will all four be sisters. And the Yorkshire moors in spring and summer are so beautiful, and my governess will be yours too, and… Mrs Staley will come round, and… and…" Miss Flora trailed off. It was too much for them all. Hugging and sobbing, they were simply three children together in a Victorian bedroom.

Miss Flora finally broke the miserable silence. "I am so sorry to upset you all, but I do so much want you to stay."

Anna looked at Helen, who nodded her head. Anna knew she'd guessed what she was thinking of saying next. "Miss Flora, we loved being here and helping you. You and Lady Louisa have been so kind to us and Connie too. But now there is something you must know about us. We didn't tell you everything." She took a deep breath and began. Trying her best to sound matter of fact, she told of how she and Helen found themselves in Victorian times. And so now they must find their way back to their own time.

Anna's heart pounded fast as she waited for Miss Flora to answer.

"If you had said that before I would have thought you mad," she said eventually. "No one in their right mind could have come up with the plan to capture Lady Dorothy as you did. I don't understand about things I cannot see and touch, but I trust you with all my heart."

"Thank you," said Anna. "I think we need to talk to Connie now. She must make her own mind up as to what she wants to do."

"Yes, you are right. We will go together. I would like to do the talking. It is my duty." Not waiting for a reply and holding her head high, Miss Flora turned and walked back into the hallway. The twins followed her silently to Connie's room. Miss Flora knocked on the door, and they all went in. Connie was looking bright and cheerful, sitting on a chair reading a book. She looked up and smiled, but her smile began to fade as they approached her.

"I hoped to see you all better now, but you look as if you have been crying."

"Connie, Miss Flora has something important to say," said Anna.

Miss Flora thanked Connie for her part in the rescue then slowly and carefully repeated what she had said to the twins. "Anna and Helen have told me why they must go. But we could give you a home here."

"That is so kind, but—"

"Please hear me out. My Mama would be the mother you lost, and I will be a sister to you." Stopping briefly to wipe a new tear away, Miss Flora blinked several times. "I am sure your Mama would be pleased that you have a home. You don't have to search for someone to love you. We love you already."

Anna took hold of Connie's hand. "We will miss you so, but now you have a chance of a home." Helen started to cry again.

It was all too much for Connie. Covering her face, she too began to cry.

After what seemed like an age, she lifted her head. "I have never known such kindness – except for Mother – but I cannot stay. I must go back and find the person who stole my mother's purse."

"Are you sure?" Anna asked.

"It would be so easy to stay, but I must take the hard path to find what is really right," Connie replied.

"That was said by a true lady. A brave speech, and we honour you," Miss Flora said.

Anna turned to Helen. "So, are we agreed then? We tell Lady Louisa now?" She fought back a new set of tears.

"If it has to be," Miss Flora replied, "then it is better said straight away."

"It will be hard having to say it," Anna said with a deep sigh. "We will miss you and everything here – even Mrs Staley."

Everyone smiled just a little bit. It helped.

Anna took hold of her sister's hand. "I'm sorry."

"What for?"

"You know you said if we told Lady Louisa everything then she could get Stoats to give us a lift?"

"Oh yes, I remember," Helen replied.

"And then I said something like it's not like catching a bus. A carriage is seen by people. We must get back in a way that no one sees?"

"Yes."

"Well… I have changed my mind. We could go back in a carriage, but by night, and Helen… I am sorry about being a clever-clog. Thinking I know the answer for everything."

"Well, I might be a dizzy-head sometimes, but just now and then a light comes on in my brain. Then it goes out again."

They couldn't help but laugh a little.

"Well now. We're feeling a bit better. Afternoon tea, everyone? Buttery crumpets, fancy cakes, little sandwiches… our last one. Oh well," Helen sighed.

"Then we tell Lady Louisa, yes?" said Connie, looking at Miss Flora.

"Of course. I shall tell Mama to wait until then. But before tea we all must wash our faces."

# Chapter Seventeen

After tea, Helen gave a long, deep sigh of satisfaction. "That was lovely, Lady Louisa."

"I am so pleased. You certainly deserved it. As to your decision for your future, Flora has asked me to wait. I am happy to listen now."

"Lady Louisa," Anna began with a slight nervous cough. "First of all, thank you so very much for your kindness to us. But we cannot stay. Miss Flora knows why."

Anna went on to tell Lady Louisa their story, and Connie told hers.

Lady Louisa sat back, looking amazed. "Well, this is one of the most extraordinary things I have ever heard. Anna and Helen, you have proved worthy with all you have done. Such bravery!

Connie, you have trusted your friends. All I can say is this: be faithful to what you believe. I am the better for knowing you all."

Anna, her voice breaking again, managed another thank you. Helen and Connie studied their plates, a few silent tears dripping down their chins. "I would like to ask… your ladyship, if we could… go back in a carriage, but by night, and then stop outside Keighley? If—"

"You mean, if Stoats would take you all?"

"Yes please."

"Yes, but you must not get into any danger when you get there. Please be careful."

"We will."

"And I suggest you get up early in the morning while it is still dark, when the maids get up. They will give you breakfast before you go."

"Mama, can I go too, just to say goodbye? Then Stoats can bring me back."

"I know I should say that you should rest, but it would be cruel not to let you go – so yes."

Miss Flora grinned. "Thank you, Mama."

After Lady Louisa left the four of them looked at each other, nobody sure what to say.

"Oh, let's not be mournful. We have the rest of the day to ourselves, so let's enjoy it," Miss Flora said.

"I would love to see the summer house," said Connie.

"Of course, you haven't seen it, have you?" Miss Flora replied. "And I will show you the wishing well too. I can face it now."

A very happy afternoon was spent in the garden. Running, chasing, playing hide and seek, acting out stories; simple, ordinary things. The time went very quickly. The winter afternoon sun soon began to die, and with it a feeling of sadness crept over them all. There was only one last dinner to eat, and then it would be bedtime.

Dinner was eaten in silence.

"We will have to sort our things out," said Anna after the meal was over and the empty dishes taken away.

"Yes," Connie replied.

Helen just nodded, her face sad.

"Please wear the clothes you are in, and put a blanket over your knees," Lady Louisa said. "It will help you to keep safe. Less chance of... well, it will look as if you are just travelling somewhere."

"Thank you, Lady Louisa," said Helen, brightening a little.

"Yes, thank you. Can we take our old clothes with us?" Anna added. "We might need them."

"Of course, give them to the maid to press and hang up – but remember you are now young ladies."

"We will," Helen said enthusiastically.

"And now I will leave you to talk. I have some letters to write."

Miss Flora waited until her mother had left. "Mama will go to her room now. It is only there that she allows herself to be sad. She has so much dignity; I have much to learn." She sighed. "So, this is your last evening in Wishwell Hall. Do you know how to play charades?"

"Yes," Anna and Helen answered together.

"We have played it sometimes at Christmas," said Helen.

"I don't," said Connie. "We were always too tired to play games."

"We will show you," Helen replied.

Connie was a quick learner, and they enjoyed a pleasant evening acting out words and phrases until they found themselves yawning and longing for their beds. "God bless and keep us all," said Miss

Flora as they hugged one another and went off to their own rooms.

The twins took their maid uniforms from under their pillows and put them out on the landing for the maid to press, then they undressed and climbed into their own beds after taking one last look round at their beautiful bedroom.

Both girls knew tomorrow would come too soon.

# Chapter Eighteen

It felt like only a few minutes had passed when there was a knock on the door. Anna opened her eyes to see the maid coming in with their breakfast. Helen must have heard, as she came through and sat on Anna's bed.

"Madam asked me to put tha'… your… old clothes in a travelling bag. They are pressed. Renton will put 'em… them… in the carriage."

"Thank you," Anna said, her heart lurching inside her.

Blushing slightly, the maid left.

"The very last breakfast," said Helen, sighing deeply. She looked at the food, laid out on a beautifully patterned wooden tray. "But at least the adventure isn't over yet."

Anna didn't reply. She had a feeling the most difficult part was still to come.

When they were full up, washed and dressed, they went downstairs to the hall where they had agreed to meet Connie and Miss Flora, who were already there. "Stoats has been told. The carriage is outside. Mama will wave to us from her bedroom window," Miss Flora said, her voice sounding flat.

Anna nodded, trying to look in control and noticing Connie and Helen looking down at the floor. "I must go and tell him exactly where to go when we arrive in Keighley," she said, making for the door.

A few moments later she was back. "It's done. We can go."

Miss Flora got into the carriage first, followed by Connie and Helen, who still hadn't spoken a word, then Anna. Miss Flora gave the order, and they were off, all waving to Lady Louisa who stood at her window holding a candle.

Anna looked inside the travelling bag. Their maid clothes were there, pressed and neatly folded up. She closed the bag and sat back, relieved. As the carriage made its way out of the grounds of Wishwell Hall, she glanced around at the others. Miss Flora sat with her eyes closed. Connie, who was sitting next to Miss Flora, seemed lost in thought. Helen was looking out of the window. Usually, she could guess what her sister was thinking, but not now.

It had been an adventure. Helen was right – it wasn't over yet. She closed her eyes, and picture memories of the time before Wishwell Hall started to float through her mind.

First it was Mrs Dreary. She could hear her now. *"You both look a bit small to be old enough for maids."*

Then seeing the purse and its contents for the first time. A necklace, a lace handkerchief, a green ribbon, a bird's feather, a lock of hair, a small flat pebble, and a folded piece of paper. She could remember them all.

Then the mill owner. *"He is not a good man. He hits people…"*

Then the old, bent-over woman. *"Aye, lass, thee won't find work now, not you with a face like a jellied eel."*

Then meeting Uncle Barney. *"Uncle Barney does no stealin' now. Uncle Barney does charity."* And the man at the back. *"Don't mind waiting."*

Then the foreign man who gave directions to Maccle. *"It not far."*

The lady at the barge came next. *"So, just close yer eyes, an' I'll tell yer a yarn. A bit of a nap before yer eat, eh?"*

Then that musty smell, her mouth being covered and much later waking up in an unfamiliar wagon. Then Minnie, who would have given them jobs at the circus.

There they all were. Any one of them could have been thieves, even Mrs Dreary – she could have followed them. One of them was. Oh, how silly she would feel if she was wrong. How much worse for Connie, who would not know what to do next. "I have to be right," she said out loud.

"What?" said Helen, turning to look at her sister. "You made me jump."

"Oh, nothing, just thinking aloud."

"I think I know what Anna was thinking," said Connie. "It's alright, you know. I won't blame you. Go to sleep like Miss Flora. You are tired."

Anna said a grateful thank you and closed her eyes again. The sound of the horse's hooves clopping the ground was so soothing…

About two hours later little birds began chirping and the sky was less dark. As the sun woke to a new day, Anna was still asleep.

She woke suddenly to a noise outside the carriage. It only took a little while to remember where she was. Had the others been asleep? She didn't know, but they were awake now. Looking out of the window, she recognised some of the streets. They were in Keighley. It was now up to Stoats to remember where to go. She watched for the curve in the road – yes, it was the right way to the street she knew so well.

Stoats brought the carriage to a halt, and Anna picked up the travelling case.

"But this is—" Helen began.

"Yes," Anna replied quickly. "Hush, we mustn't make any noise."

They had arrived at a house Helen knew well.

Grandma's house.

"Miss Flora, will you knock on the door, please?" Anna whispered.

"Yes, of course, who do I ask for?"

"The master of the house."

Miss Flora walked up the steps and knocked on the door. A few moments later it was opened, to Anna's relief, by Mrs Dreary. Clearly, she was still the housekeeper. It was clear from the blank look on her face that she had no idea who they were.

"I am Miss Flora of Wishwell Hall. Can I see your master, please?"

"The master? Oh… the master…"

"We wish to speak to him."

"Oh, ah… yes, please come in."

Anna watched as Mrs Dreary glanced at the carriage then beckoned them in nervously. "If you will wait in here, I shall tell the master." She showed them into the parlour and then hurried away, closing the door behind her.

As soon as she was gone, Helen turned to her sister. "Her master will come, and then she will be caught. I knew it would be her. Then Connie will get her necklace back, and then we can ask Stoats to find Maccle for us, and then we—"

"Be quiet," snapped Anna.

Helen stopped, her cheeks flushing with anger.

This was it. Anna felt her heart begin to beat faster.

A few minutes later the sound of footsteps approaching made everyone stare at the door. Anna guessed the others would be wondering who it could be. Her mouth went dry as once more she found herself thinking how silly she would look and how ashamed she would be if she was wrong.

The door opened, and Mrs Dreary came in, followed by the master of the house. Connie gasped. It was the mill owner himself! Mr Cooper.

Mrs Dreary slipped out quietly, leaving everyone standing in tense silence. "You!" said the master, glaring at Connie. "What's with those new clothes? And who are all of you?" He stared at each of them, frowning.

Anna took a step closer before Miss Flora could answer. "You stole Connie's necklace, the one in the purse, and we want it back. You had to lie low for a few days. You couldn't just disappear – it would look as if you had started the fire."

He narrowed his eyes. "So you think that, do you?"

"Yes," said Connie. "I don't know how my friend knows this. I don't know how she knew where you would be. But she is telling the truth."

There was no answer.

Anna waited, not moving, fixing her eyes straight ahead.

# Chapter Nineteen

As Anna watched, a slow smile crept over Mr Cooper's face and widened. Then he broke into a laugh.

"You might think that's funny," said Helen, coming to her sister's side, "but we don't."

"Yes, alright then. It was me who stole it. I'm not afraid of *you*. Children, that's all you are. I heard you all talking on the hill. I saw what was in the purse. I saw you before you saw me. How did you know it was me, anyway?"

Connie mumbled something about everyone knowing the master was a bad lot.

"Yes," said Anna, "but also you are left-handed like me. When you tried to poison us, it was your left hand on my face. I didn't guess it until I wanted to sneeze later that day. Because I didn't have a handkerchief, I tried to stop it by putting my hand over my mouth…"

"It was just to knock you out, not kill you. I ditched you at the circus, hoping you would join it, travel the country and not come back."

"Well, we didn't, and when I sneezed the feeling of my hand over my mouth brought it all back. I could tell then it must have been a left-handed person, like me. And you."

"Clever, yes. I am left-handed."

"You followed us. You were the man at the back of the pawn shop and the man who gave me directions to Maccle. You were in disguise."

"How did you know?"

"When my cap blew away you stopped it with your foot. You picked it up and gave it to me with your left hand. I didn't notice it then; it wasn't until later when I got to think. I notice people who are left-handed like me, you see. And also, we have been here before."

"When?"

"I am not saying when, but I noticed your hat stand is on the left side of the door in the hall."

"You are clever, for a girl."

"Yes, she is, and she is my friend... and I want my mother's things," said Connie, finding her voice.

Mr Cooper laughed harshly. "You think the necklace is worth something, do you? Here you are, then." He reached into his jacket pocket, drew out the purse, and threw it at Connie.

She opened it and drew out the necklace. "Well, here it is."

Crowding round Connie, Miss Flora, Anna, and Helen gazed at it.

"Sparkles, doesn't it?" Connie said.

"Oh, it does that alright."

"Check that everything is there," suggested Miss Flora.

Connie poured the contents out. Along with the necklace was a lace handkerchief, a bird's feather, a lock of hair, and a folded piece of paper. "Is that everything?" Miss Flora asked.

"Yes, I think so. There was a green ribbon, but we sold it."

"Right, take your purse and go," said Mr Cooper, turning to the door and looking as if he was in a hurry to get rid of them. They gathered up Connie's things and made to leave.

Anna suddenly stopped. "There was something else! I remember now – a small pebble."

"Oh, yes," said Connie. "I remember it too. It felt nice. Mother must have kept it for a reason."

Mr Cooper stopped in the open doorway. He turned back towards them, muttering to himself, "Why not? It would be fun." He reached into his pocket, took something out, and opened his hand.

The pebble.

He grinned. "Do you mean this, eh? A pebble? So that's it, is it, just a pebble?" He threw his head back and laughed. "I don't suppose you have seen a diamond before, eh?"

"What, that thing?" huffed Helen.

"This is an uncut diamond. I was a miner once. That's what they look like before they are polished. I have seen many diamonds but only one like this. This is a *maccle* – a very special diamond."

Everyone stared at the pebble in disbelief.

"I recognised it when I saw it, as they are small, flat and triangle-shaped. This is a rare one, and it's worth a fortune. Nothing like your precious necklace. That might get you a few coins, but that's all."

"So Maccle wasn't a place after all?" whispered Anna.

"My mother must have known that. She was keeping it to... to make me a lady," said Connie.

Mr Cooper said, "I heard you talking about 'May', by the way, when you were on the hill. That must be Lord May, who lived in Atwood Lodge, a few miles away. I expect that was what your mother was trying to tell you. No good looking for him now – he died yesterday. His butler is my cousin."

"My grandfather. That's who it must be. So, he is dead. Mother must have hoped he would help me." Connie sighed. "I cannot feel anything. He did nothing to find me."

Despite Connie's words, Anna saw tears gathering in her eyes and put her arm around her shoulder.

"So, you see," continued Mr Cooper, "when I saw the maccle, I had to lure you away. That diamond would set me up for life. And yes, I had to lie low, but I have my contacts. I will be out of the country by next week."

"Oh, no, you won't," said Miss Flora. "I am Miss Flora of Wishwell Hall, and I have my carriage and coachman outside."

In a second Mr Cooper was off through the hall and through the front door, dashing into the road. Anna, Helen, and Connie sprinted after him, and Miss Flora ran to Stoats, calling out, "After him! He is a diamond thief!"

Stoats jumped down off his horse then ran off in pursuit of Mr Cooper, soon outrunning Miss Flora and the others. But Mr Cooper was a strong man and looked as if he was getting away. Stoats, an older man, could not catch him up.

It wasn't long before the girls had to stop. They could only watch breathlessly as Stoats continued running, but the gap between him and Mr Cooper was widening. "He's not going to catch him," panted Helen.

"No, but we are. Quick! Back to the horse and carriage, no questions." Miss Flora sprinted back up the hill to the carriage, and the others followed, gasping for breath. "Get in!" she ordered. "We are *not* letting him get away."

The three of them bundled in. "Close the door. I am going to drive," Miss Flora shouted, disappearing. The next thing they knew they were racing down the hill, tumbling into one another as they were thrown about. They could see nothing in front. It was nerve racking and exhilarating all at the same time.

Gathering speed, they were soon careering into the main part of town. Groups of people, adults and children with blank, downturned faces, were making their way to work. Mr Cooper ran towards them, making them part in the middle and then crowd back together, Stoats forcing his way through in his wake. "Stop, thief!" he bellowed, and the crowd stared at him, but no one bothered to give chase.

The carriage swerved even more as they followed Mr Cooper down alleys and side streets. Stoats had been left far behind. One sharp bend in the road and Miss Flora nearly lost control. Another even sharper bend and they nearly toppled over. The sound of the horse's hooves pounding on the cobbles echoed through the carriage. The three girls clung to each other, clasping hands, keeping one another steady.

Faster still they went. A dog in the street began to give chase, barking wildly and dashing into the road under the horse's hooves. The horse whinnied desperately and, in just a few seconds, the girls were thrown into the air. The carriage toppled over with a loud crash. Anna grabbed Helen's hand. She tried to reach out for Connie, but something would not let her. She tried again but couldn't; something was pulling her back – and it was too strong for her.

Someone was calling her name, then Helen's. "Anna... Helen... is that you two down there?"

Again it came, only this time louder. "Anna! Helen! Is that you two?"

Grandma? *No!* Anna squeezed her eyes closed. They must not go back, not now, not without knowing what would happen to Miss Flora and Connie and the diamond.

It was no use. The voice was getting louder. Anna opened her eyes, and there she was, holding hands with Helen in Grandma's kitchen. Opposite them was a fridge. The trunk was there by the door. They looked at each other. They were wearing the clothes they wore on the day they had decided to go skating on the lake.

The shock was too much for them both. They could not speak. Grandma's footsteps on the stairs were getting closer. All they could do was stand there, watching as the door handle turned.

Grandma stood in the doorway, frowning at them. "I thought I heard a crash. Whatever is the matter?"

"The trunk," Anna managed to gasp. "Grandma, it was the trunk."

Grandma gazed at her. "Oh! So I was right. All those years ago. Well now."

"Grandma, we have… been … it's all…"

"Strange? I know. Tell me all about it."

# Chapter Twenty

Anna and Helen told Grandma everything – every incredible bit. They stumbled over their words, and cried, and now they felt exhausted. "We're not making it up, Grandma," Helen managed to say as they came to the end.

Grandma smiled. "I believe every word. I told you the trunk was already here when I came to live in the house, didn't I? It was just part of the kitchen?"

"Yes, we remember," said Anna.

"Everything that has just happened and what you've said has brought back a memory. After I was married and just moved in, I thought I would have a good look in the trunk. I was a new bride then."

A sudden fall of heavy snow outside made her stop talking for a minute and stare out of the window.

"I took a few dresses out and held them to my body. For a few moments I felt strange, as though someone needed me from… I didn't know where. I quickly put them all back. I told myself not to be silly. I then forgot all about it. So, now I know why."

"Grandma, now we are back here, we don't why and what happened to them," Helen said sadly.

"Yes, but it is not for us to know the future."

"But it's not. It's the past," said Anna.

"But for them it would be the future, the beginning of it anyway."

"I don't get it," said Helen.

Grandma nodded. "It's a lot to take in. But maybe there is a way of finding out what happened. We could try the church… only the old vicar has just retired. We have a new one now, so he may not know if they are—"

"You're going to say alive, aren't you?" Anna said.

"Yes. Now, you two think carefully. Do you want to do this, even if things didn't turn out well?"

"Yes," Anna and Helen replied, both at the same time.

"We need to know," said Anna.

"Then let's go. But before we do I want my breakfast. I reckon you've had yours?"

Anna and Helen both looked down.

"Don't tell me, hoping to escape before anyone woke up? Skating, perhaps? Your mum does fuss a bit, but I'm on your side. Give me a quarter of an hour, and I'll be ready."

# Chapter Twenty-One

Dressed for the cold, they followed their grandma outside into the newly laid snow. The church was normally only a few minutes' walk from the house, but it took longer in the snow, slipping and sliding and trying to keep themselves from falling. Holding hands helped, especially as a wind was getting up.

They talked only twice. Once was Grandma saying that the vicar had rung yesterday to say the service was cancelled due to the snow, and the second was Anna asking if the church would be open. Grandma nodded, looking as if she knew for certain it would be.

Fortunately, it was. It was a relief to get out of the wind. "Now, where do we begin?" Grandma whispered, glancing around. "How about we look at the plaques on the wall? There might be something. Funny, I've never looked at them properly before. Still, how about we take one wall each?"

Each of them walked the full length of their chosen wall, reading everything carefully. A few minutes later they met back where they had started. "Found anything?" Grandma asked. Anna shook her head, as did Helen. "Me neither. We could try reading the inscriptions on the floor."

"Oh, yes. I saw a few of those," Anna replied. "There's one here."

They were so busy bending down they didn't see a man come out of a room at the front of the church and start walking towards them. Hearing footsteps, they all looked up.

"Sorry to startle you, but I thought I heard something. I am the new vicar, not been here long. Awful weather, so much snow, that's why I had to cancel the service. You all look as if you like history. This church has a fascinating past."

The face smiling at them was young and rather handsome. Helen was the first to speak. "Oh, we do. This is my sister Anna, and we are twins, and this lady here is my grandma, and we came to stay for Christmas, and now because of the snow we can't go home…" she trailed off.

"Oh, yes, of course. How brave of you to have walked here. Now, as I was saying…" The vicar was not to be put off. Various examples of early Perpendicular Gothic styles, followed with something about pointed arches, which made Anna think about feet, were shown with great delight. Then more early history stuff, which was so boring they stopped listening.

Anna tried coughing at certain intervals. Grandma did too. Even Helen gave up smiling and began rubbing her hands together. Eventually it worked. "Oh, I'm talking away, and with the cold air in here. Can't have you all going down with flu in the new year. Come and have a cup of tea in the vestry."

Gratefully they followed him into the room at the front, which was a bit warmer but not much, and sat down on some old wooden chairs. He busied himself making a pot of tea, letting it brew for only a few seconds before pouring it out and handing cups round. Anna noticed it looked very weak.

"Sorry about all these cardboard boxes. The last vicar was a hoarder. Mind you, he was well respected. He retired, good age too. Over the years he collected a lot of local history stuff. I had a quick look. Some of it is quite interesting."

"Oh, that's good," Anna said, trying her best to smile. "I mean, that's about people who live here, yes? We are looking—"

"Yes," Helen chipped in, not wanting to be outdone. "We are trying to... no, er... we are interested in someone who might have lived nearby... a sort of relative..."

"What my granddaughters mean is they would like to find out about someone who lived here in the last century."

The vicar beamed. "It's a rare thing to see children so interested in history. It has made my day. You're very welcome to have a hunt through these boxes. But finish your tea first."

They both gulped their tea down, Helen almost choking.

"Well, I will leave you to it," said the vicar, rising from his chair.

"And do you mind if I leave them to it as well?" Grandma said. "I'll wait for them at the back of church."

"Of course not, nothing to pinch in here." He chuckled to himself. He turned in the doorway. "Hope you find what you're looking for."

"Glad he's gone," Anna said when Grandma and the vicar had left. "I'm up to here in early perpendiculars, whatever they are."

"Oh, but didn't he say it nicely?" Helen sighed.

"Come on, dreamy eyes. We have some boxes to go through."

"I know, but just look at that pile."

All the cardboard boxes had been piled up in one corner of the room opposite the desk. They were all sorts of shapes and sizes, stacked so high they almost touched the ceiling.

"We'll have to stand on a chair to lift them down," Anna said.

"This is where I really break my ankle," Helen laughed. "Right. I'll climb first, then we take it in turns."

Anna scraped one of the chairs over and Helen climbed onto it. She reached out carefully, lifting the top box and passing it down to Anna. It wasn't too heavy. She dusted herself down as she jumped to the floor, watching Anna open the box.

It was packed with photos, thank you cards, and newspaper cuttings, mostly modern, nothing Victorian.

They did the same with the next three boxes. There was nothing interesting in them, either.

The next box looked similar, but at least its contents were a good few years older than the stuff in the first few boxes. "Phew, my arms are killing me," Helen said.

"Me too," said Anna, "but at least the pile is getting smaller, only five more to go. Look – if we push our backs against the top two, we might be able to bump them down. Doubt there's anything breakable in any of them."

"Fine by me," replied Helen, shaking both arms to get the feeling back in them.

Together they managed to shove the boxes without too much effort. All five boxes were now lined up in a row, ready to be searched. "There's got to be something in one of them," said Helen.

"Yes," sighed Anna. "If there isn't, then I don't know what we shall do."

"I'll cry or have a tantrum or something."

"Tell you what," said Anna, sounding braver than she felt, "You take the one at that end, and I'll take the one at the other end, then we'll meet in the middle."

"Right," said Helen, shuffling over to one end of the row. "Curtain up, sister. Final performance."

"Hope so," replied Anna, grabbing her box. "I really do."

# Chapter Twenty-Two

Counting to ten, together they opened the box in front of them and began to rummage through.

"Newspaper cuttings, thank you cards, funeral programmes, wedding programmes, more of the same," Anna said.

"And me, but I've not got to the bottom yet. Ah… something a bit better. Here's a bundle of letters." Helen scoured the envelopes and sighed. "No, just bills. Here we go again – more thank you cards, oh, and one more letter – another bill, I guess." Helen fished out the envelope and turned it over. "Anna!" she suddenly cried out. "Tell me, am I seeing right?"

Anna hurried across to Helen and stared over her shoulder. There in front of her, in thin spiky writing, were the words 'For the attention of Anna and Helen Price'.

"That's us! It has to be," Helen whispered. "There can't be anybody in Keighley with our names. We don't come from round here."

Anna nodded. "Shall I open it, or you? No… you open it, it was in your box."

With trembling fingers Helen edged the sticky bit at the back of the envelope open. Slowly she took out the letter, unfolded it and laid it flat on her knees where they could both see it clearly. At the top right was the address, a hospital; and underneath was the date, 1929. Then the words: 'Dear Anna and Helen…'

"It *is* us," Helen said, her voice cracking. "I mustn't cry. Don't let me cry. I mustn't get it wet. Here, you read it to me. Take it. I daren't touch it."

Reaching across to Helen's lap, Anna carefully took hold of the letter. Taking a big deep breath to calm herself down, she began to read it aloud. "Dear Anna and Helen, I am an old lady now, and they say I haven't much longer to live. You might want to know what happened to me after you went. If the good Lord sees fit, then I will pass this letter onto the vicar to keep it safe. Pray Lord it will get to you—"

"It has to be Connie," Helen cried.

"Hush, you don't want the vicar to hear, do you?"

Helen shook her head.

Anna continued to read. "You remember, Anna, in the carriage when the horse made that loud cry? We were thrown into the air. I tried to grab your hand, but I couldn't reach you. I knew you were near, but then I banged my head, and it made me dizzy. When it stopped, you and Helen had gone. Then there were people running, and it was all a jumble, and I fainted. I found out later that Miss Flora had been thrown clear off her horse. It was a miracle that she was alright – thankfully she landed on some grass near the road. Then someone came dashing over, saying that the master had dropped down dead in the street. The police came. It was true – he had died. It must have been the running that finished him off. The diamond was still in his pocket."

"Good riddance," said Helen.

"Do you want to read the rest of it now you're feeling better?" Anna asked.

"No, just in case... no, carry on."

Anna swallowed and began again. "Lady Louisa saw to everything for me. She arranged for my mother to be buried in the churchyard. The diamond was sold. The money was put in a trust fund until I was twenty-one. I wanted to live in the master's house, because it was near enough for me to walk to Mother's grave, but I was too young to be on my own, so Lady Louisa bought the house, and it was let out. I went to live with her and Miss Flora."

"Oh, how wonderful! She became a lady. Just think... all those afternoon teas and that footman," Helen sighed.

Anna grinned. "Are you sure you don't want to read?"

Helen shook her head.

"In that case, listen if you want me to read the rest."

"Sorry, I won't say another word."

Anna continued. "Lady Louisa had Mother's furniture brought round to the house. There wasn't a lot. The biggest thing was her trunk with all her nice dresses, which she'd had in Africa. Your maid clothes from the travelling bag were put in it. I wanted to keep them. It was all I had left of you both. It was put in the kitchen because that was where the sun shone the most. Mother loved the sun because it reminded her of Africa—"

"Oh, that's why the trunk was in the kitchen!" Helen exclaimed. "Sorry! Promised I wouldn't talk."

"It's alright, I need to stop for a minute anyway. I'm getting hoarse."

It was fortunate for them both, as just at that moment the vicar opened the door and came in. He looked at the boxes on the floor. "You've been busy, then. Did you find what you were looking for?"

"Yes," Helen replied. "We have found a letter from Con… our… relative, who we were looking for. We are reading it now."

"Oh, I am pleased. Now, my wife told me off for using old tea, and she has given me some coffee and biscuits. Sorry, and you being so interested in history too. Would you like some?"

"Oh, yes please," said Helen, giving her best smile ever.

"Good. And by the way, your grandma is waiting for you in the vicarage. It's warmer there."

A few minutes later, after a welcome break for coffee and biscuits, the vicar left. "I needed that," said Anna. "My voice is better now. I'll carry on reading. Where was I?"

"The bit about the trunk being put in the kitchen."

"Oh, yes, I've found it. Here goes." Anna paused and took a deep breath. "The years went by, and they were lovely, growing up with Miss Flora who became like a sister to me. When I turned twenty-one the money came to me. It was more than I could have ever dreamed of having. I could afford to buy a mansion, but I felt something was telling me 'no'. I paid back the money for the master's old house, and I went to live in it."

"So she lived in Grandma's house, not knowing one day in the future we would visit," Helen said.

"Yes. It's like time went wobbly, not straight. Anyway, there's still some more to read." Anna lowered her head. "I missed being with Miss Flora and Lady Louisa, but it was good to be back in Keighley. I visited my mother's grave every day. One day when I was kneeling by her grave, I heard a little girl crying. I got up and went to her. She said she had lost her mummy, and I helped her find her. It made me think about all the little children who were lost. As I was thinking, the words on that little bit of paper in Mother's purse came into my mind. Do you remember? 'In all your ways acknowledge Him, and He shall direct your paths. Proverbs 3 verse 6.' I heard it in my head, and I knew that God wanted me to help little African babies. So I went to

Africa, and that is what I did. I worked in an orphanage. One of the things I did was to rescue twins, because bad things sometimes happened to them. It became my life's work. I didn't want the money from the diamond, so I gave it away. I found peace in Africa. I only came back to England because I became ill. I have loved my life. The real treasure in Mother's purse was the bit of paper, not the diamond. I hope you both find real treasure too. I am tired now…"

Anna suddenly stopped.

"And?" said Helen.

"There's no more."

"What about the other side?"

Anna turned the page over. "Oh, there is some writing on the back, but it's not Connie's. It says: 'Connie Abara died two days after writing this letter. She is buried at the side of the churchyard opposite the tower and next to her mother, at her own request.'" Anna quietly folded the letter back into the envelope and looked at her sister. Together they hugged and cried, their tears mingling as one.

"We need to find her," Anna managed to say after a few minutes had gone by.

"Yes," Helen replied, rubbing her coat sleeve over her eyes.

Silently they made their way outside, holding hands, and walked round to the side of the church. The path was icy in places, and once or twice they nearly slipped but managed to catch themselves in time. They stopped next to the tower near a long row of graves. Some headstones were completely covered in snow. The larger ones stuck out, grey above white.

Still holding hands, they trudged towards the first gravestone. Brushing the snow away, they read the inscription. It wasn't Connie or her mother. They tried the next one and the next, but they weren't either.

The next one was Connie's mother's grave.

Gripping their hands together even tighter, they brushed the snow away on the next stone.

There it was.

> Connie Abara
> Born 1852
> Died 1929
>
> In all your ways acknowledge Him,
> and He shall direct your paths.
> Proverbs 3v6

There were no tears, only a sense of great peace as they looked at the place where their friend was buried.

"We are not the same, me and you," Anna whispered.

"No."

"There's only one thing left to do now."

Facing each other, they both knew what it was. Together, and very carefully, they pushed the snow away from the grave. Then, in the snowy silence of the crisp morning, they knelt in front of it and closed their eyes. Taking it in turns, they simply said thank you for their friend. As they stood up, they gazed at the grave and one another, not wanting to go, sensing the oneness that twins often feel, and they knew that Connie had found a true home.

She was no longer lost.

They didn't hear Grandma until she was almost behind them. They turned to her. "We found a letter with our names on. It's from Connie," Anna whispered, her breath visible in the icy air.

"So, you know everything now."

"Yes. It's her... handwriting, and..." Helen stopped, not able to form any more words.

Grandma smiled gently and patted her hand. "Keep it safe. A person's handwriting is precious. I am old enough to know that."

Anna and Helen said nothing more. They turned back to the grave. It was hard to say goodbye.

After a few silent moments, Anna felt her grandma's arms around her, wrapping her and her sister tightly into her embrace. Grandma stepped back and rested her hand on their shoulders, then silently led them away.

## The End

# Some Helpful History

The winter of 1962-63 was one of the coldest Britain has known. Snow began to fall on Boxing Day 1962 and did not stop for the next ten weeks.

Can you imagine a time when snow lay on the ground for more than 60 days? Can you imagine the temperature barely climbing above freezing for three whole months? That was what it was like for people living then.

Most people in those days didn't have central heating. Often there was only one coal fire in the living room. Imagine how cold the house would be!

## Fridges

In the 1950s, refrigerators, or 'fridges' as they are now known, became a part of the modern kitchen for some people.

By the 1960s many more people could afford one. Today nearly everyone has a fridge in their kitchen.

## Servants

In Victorian times lots of well-to-do houses had servants to run the house. But they were expected to stay out of sight and use the back stairs. Lots of poorer people worked as servants.

## Victorian Cotton and Woollen Mills

Lots of young girls worked in mills. Little fingers could reach in between the moving machinery and mend broken threads. The girls were also small enough to crawl underneath to pick up bits of wool and cotton. Sometimes hair or fingers got caught in the machinery.

The mills were also hot and noisy. People had to shout above the noise of the machinery, causing deafness. Often children fell asleep, as it was a long day. Many children died before the age of sixteen.

## The Mill Owner

The mill owner ran his factory to make as much money as possible. Often workers had to obey strict rules and received harsh punishments. Many factory owners lived in large, comfortable houses. Many would have held tea parties and invited well-off guests. The mill owner was the big boss; no one argued with him. Some were kinder and tried to give the people who worked for them better working conditions.

## The Pawnbroker

These were often known as 'Uncle'. He was always there in times of need and provided loans for all sorts of things found in the home.

The entrance to a pawnbroker's shop was usually in a side street. The pawnbroker was often the means to buy food for the family when the cupboard was bare.

If the items were not collected the pawnbroker was allowed to keep them and sell them after one year and seven days.

## Escaped Lion (Yes, it has happened for real!)

It is a warm June afternoon in 1889. In the drawing room of a hotel in Wales Mr T.J. Osborne is packing to go home. The window is open when a fully-grown African lion leaps in. Mr Osborne grabs a chair and is ready to defend himself.

Fortunately, the lion's keeper and his assistants arrive from the site of Wombwell's Menagerie, which is parked nearby.

"Don't move an inch," the keeper says to Mr. Osborne.

Mr. Osborne obeys and stands still as the lion paces the room. Slowly and carefully the keeper and his staff close in on the lion and fling a sack over its head. They then secure it with ropes. The lion is caught. Mr. Osborne is safe!

## Victorian barges

A barge was a type of boat that was used for transporting goods. They were used on canals and were pulled along by a horse who walked on the path.

## The Victorian circus

A circus parade took its wagons with caged lions, camels, horses, and elephants through town for all to see. Circuses in Victorian times were held either in a small tent or in the open air. The circus did include child performers. Tick riding was an important performance at every circus in Britain. Other acts changed from circus to circus.

## Orf chump

Someone with no appetite.

## Wishing well

It was thought that any spoken wish would be granted when you threw a coin into the well.

## Maccle

No one knows the correct spelling for maccle – it could be 'macle', 'maccle', 'maacle', or 'mackle'. It has changed over time. But there is one thing that is certain: a maccle is a rough diamond used to make fancy jewellery that is very beautiful. Sometimes hearts are made from maccles. They can cost a lot of money to buy.

# About the Author

Anne Jordan lives in Leicestershire with her husband Paul. After becoming a Christian in her teens, Anne trained to be a primary teacher. After her children left home, she became an Adult Education Tutor, teaching people with learning difficulties and disabilities. She also taught creative writing to a class of adults who were recovering from mental health problems.

Anne is now retired but has a heart for vulnerable children as well as a love of history. She hopes you enjoyed reading this book.

This book is dedicated to Home for Good, a Christian charity with a Biblical mandate to care for vulnerable children.

Home for Good is dedicated to finding a home for every child who needs one.

See homeforgood.org.uk

Printed in Dunstable, United Kingdom